PREVENTING BULLYING
A Manual for Teachers in Promoting Global Educational Harmony

Raju Ramanathan, M. Tech &
Christina Theophilos, M.Ed.

Copyright © 2021 by Raju Ramanathan & Christina Theophilos, M.Ed.

All rights reserved. No part of this publication may be reproduced, distributed, or transmitted in any form or by any means, including photocopying, recording, or other electronic or mechanical methods, without the prior written permission of the publisher, except in the case brief quotations embodied in critical reviews and other noncommercial uses permitted by copyright law.

ISBN: 978-1-77759-873-0 (Paperback)
        978-1-77759-874-7 (Hardback)
        978-1-77759-875-4 (E-book)

The views expressed in this book are solely those of the author and do not necessarily reflect the views of the publisher, and the publisher hereby disclaims any responsibility for them.

Mercury Man Publishing House
www.mercurymanpublishing.com

CONTENTS

Legal & Disclaimer xi
Acknowledgments xiii
Global Educational Harmony xvi
Why Educators Need This Manual xviii
About The Authors xxiii

Section 1: BULLYING OVERVIEW   1

    Five Types of Bullying 5
    Factors Contributing to Bullying 7
    Bullying from a Lifespan Perspective 10
    Where Bullying Occurs 11
    Cyberbullying 12
    Bystanders 14
    Children at Risk 15
    Bullying Outcomes 17
    Long-Term Effects of Bullying 21

Section 2: How Schools Can Help Prevent Bullying   23

    Challenges Schools Face in Preventing Bullying 26
    Questions to Consider About Your School's
        Anti-Bullying Initiatives 28
    Seven Steps to Developing Your School's Action Plan 29
    How to Promote a Bully-Free School Environment 31
    Bullying Prevention Objectives 32
    Bullying Assessment Questionnaire 34
    Our School's Code of Conduct Form 35
    Sanctions for Misconduct Form 37
    Giving Advice to Parents About Bullying 38
    Bullying Prevention Letter to Parents 40
    Important Signs of Bullying That Parents Should Know 41
    Parenting Tips: What to Do if Your Child is Being Bullied . . 43
    How to Respond to Cyberbullying 48

Section 3: Prevention & Response Strategies For Educators   49

Questions to Consider Before Your Bullying
    Prevention Initiatives 52
Identifying Students' Needs. 54
How to Recognize Your Students' Roles in Bullying 56
The Glory of Education's 7 Step Bullying Prevention Model . . . 57
    Step 1: Set a Harmonious Tone in the Classroom 57
    Step 2: Create Respectful Ground Rules 58
    Step 3: Raise Students' Awareness about Bullying 58
    Step 4: Cultivate Moments of Empathy and Morality. . . . 59
    Step 5: Eliminate the Motivation to Bully
        by Building Peer Relations 59
    Step 6: Provide Opportunities to Practice
        Conflict Resolution and Interpersonal Skills. 60
    Step 7: Encourage Leadership by Getting Students
        Involved in the Prevention Process. 61
Activity Layout and Design. 62
Examples of Post-activity processing questions:. 63
Benefits of Classroom-Based Learning Activities. 64
The Importance of Making Random Groups 67
How to Make Random Groups. 69
Essential Facilitation Tips Before Teaching Anti-Bullying 70

Section 4: Intervention Strategies   75

Classroom Management Techniques 77
Suggestions on Setting Ground Rules 79
Using the 3 R's: Recognize, React and Resolve
    a Bullying Situation 81
How to Resolve a Bullying Situation in Class. 83
Reporting Misconduct to Authorities: "Heads Up" Form 84
Student Referral to Administration. 84
Student Misconduct Reflection Sheet 85
How to Have Meaningful Student Interventions 86
    Intervention Strategies for Bystanders 86
    Intervention Strategies for the Target. 87
    Empowering Solutions for Targets 89
    Food for Thought Before Your 1-1 Intervention with the Bully   91
Intervention Strategies for the Bully 91

    1-1 Discussion Questions for theBully 92
    When YOU, the Teacher, is a Target of Bullying 94
    How to Confront Your Bully 94
    Do YOU bully your students?. 97

Section 5: Bullying Prevention Class Activities   99

    Step 1: Set a Harmonious Tone in the Classroom. 101
        Activity #1: Create Calmness and Concentration
            Using Mindful Meditation. 102
        Activity #2: Stretch and Feel Great 105
        Activity #3: Promote Respect for Self and
            Others Using the "I Am Mantra". 109
        Activity #4: Repeat Positive Incantations 113
        Activity #5: Practice the Art of Listening and
            Identify Our Human Needs 115
        Activity #6: Establish Trust — Group Discussion and
            Action Exercises 122
        Activity #7: Sing and Automatically Feel Uplifted 127
    Step 2: Create Respectful Ground Rules 133
        Activity #8: Brainstorm Respectful Do's and Don'ts 135
        Activity #9: Appropriate Code of Conduct and
            Sanctions Forms 142
        Sanctions for Misconduct Form 146
        Activity #10: Establish Class Rules in Small Groups 148
        Activity #11: Identify Cool and Uncool Behaviors 150
    Step 3: Raise Students' Awareness about Bullying 155
        Activity #12: Define Bullying. 156
        Activity #13: Class Discussion and Questions About Bullying 162
        Activity #14: Bullying Word Associations — Icebreaker . . . 177
        Activity #15: Demystify Bullying — True or False Exercise . 181
        Activity #16: "Step Up If" — Identifying Student
            Commonalities. 192
        Activity #17: Write Your Truth About Bullying
            and Post It Anonymously 196
    Step 4: Cultivate Moments of Empathy and Morality 200
        Activity #18: Walk in Their Shoes;
            An Experiential Learning Exercise. 201
        Activity #19: Explore Bullying Roles —
            Small Group Discussion 211

Activity #20: The Use and Abuse of Power —
    Round Circle Discussion. 219
Activity #21: Understand the Effects of Bullying 222
Activity #22: Share Feelings — "I feel… when…" 234
Activity #23: Identify Students' Values —
    Discussion and Worksheet. 237
Activity #24: Student Confessions and
    Identifying Bullying Roles 240
Step 5: Eliminate the Motivation to Bully by
    Building Peer Relations 247
Activity #25: The Masks We Wear! 248
Activity #26: Find Commonalities —
    "Find Someone Who…". 251
Activity #27: "If You Really Knew Me" 253
Activity #28: Admit Your Mistakes and
    Apologize to Those You Hurt 257
Activity #29: Share Your Bullying Story and Let It Go. . . . 268
Activity #30: Forgive Vs. Holding Grudges. 271
Step 6: Provide Opportunities to Practice Conflict Resolution
  and Interpersonal Skills 276
Activity #31: Locating Bullying Hot Spots and
    How to Respond. 278
Activity #32: Improvise Bullying Response Strategies 287
Activity #33: Brainstorm Anti-Bullying Responses in
    Small Groups 290
Activity #34: Practice Makes Perfect —
    More Bullying Scenarios. 294
Activity #35: Time to Debate Bullying Topics 298
Activity #36: Give and Receive Compliments 305
Step 7: Encourage Leadership by Getting Students Involved
  in the Prevention Process 309
Activity #37: Set Appealing Goals for Their Future. 310
Activity #38: Define Authentic Leadership. 318
Activity #39: Get Students Involved in the
    Prevention Process. 321
Activity #40: Create an Anti-Bullying Skit —
    Group Project 324
Activity #41: Create Anti-Bullying Posters and Flyers 326

Activity #42: Make an Anti-Bullying Pledge and
    Certificate of Understanding. 328
Activity #43: Peer Mentoring Program 330
A FINAL MESSAGE. 332

LEGAL & DISCLAIMER

The information contained in this book and its contents is not designed to replace or take the place of any form of medical or professional advice; and is not meant to replace the need for independent medical, financial, legal or other professional advice or services, as may be required. The content and information in this book have been provided for educational and entertainment purposes only.

This teacher's manual contains practical information, inspiration, classroom-based learning activities, and teaching strategies for educators on how to prevent and respond to bullying. The use or misuse of the given content, along with any misunderstanding of the material, is the sole responsibility of the reader.

Neither the author nor the publishers assume responsibility or liability, jointly or individually, to any person, group, organization or entity regarding any emotional loss, damage, or injury, which may be caused or allegedly caused, directly or indirectly, from the information provided. The author is an educational consultant, associate professor, researcher and workshop facilitator, not a licensed psychiatrist.

As educators reading this manual, you must use your own discretion and judgment when applying the activities, interventions, and strategies provided. Readers are recommended to use the activities provided logically and safely in accordance with their teaching style and student needs. The contents can also be effective when used in conjunction with professional, or counseling services, which are related to bullying.

The content and information contained in this book has been compiled from sources deemed reliable, and it is accurate to the best of the Author's knowledge, information, and belief. However, the author cannot guarantee its accuracy and validity and cannot be held liable for any errors and/or omissions. Further, changes are periodically made to this book as and when needed. Where appropriate and/or necessary, you must consult a professional (including but not limited to your doctor, attorney, financial advisor or such other professional advisor) before using any of the suggested remedies, techniques, or information in this book.

Upon using the contents and information contained in this book, you agree to hold harmless the Author from and against any damages, costs, and expenses, including any legal fees potentially resulting from the application of any of the information provided by this book. This disclaimer applies to any loss, damages or injury caused by the use and application, whether directly or indirectly, of any advice or information presented, whether for breach of contract, tort, negligence, personal injury, criminal intent, or under any other cause of action.

You agree to accept all risks of using the information presented inside this book.

You agree that by continuing to read this book, where appropriate and/or necessary, you shall consult a professional (including but not limited to your doctor, attorney, or financial advisor or such other advisor as needed) before using any of the suggested remedies, techniques, or information in this book.

ACKNOWLEDGMENTS

To the chosen ones, who choose to devote their lives to teaching, we thank you. You have the power to make or break some of the most critical years in your students' adolescent lives. Your encouragement or discouragement in a subject can pave the way to their future success and confidence in the given field you are privileged to teach. Please remember the impact of your attitude, subtle behavior, and *expectations* you have of your students. If you believe in them, they too will believe in themselves and see the potential that lies within them. If you treat them like winners, they will become winners. But if you treat them as failures or incompetent individuals, they too will feel this way. Therefore, it is important that you keep yourself healthy, strong, and well-balanced both physically and emotionally, to uplift and inspire them daily. If you dominate their thoughts with positive and uplifting ways of being, they too will be influenced by this, in a classroom setting that you always dreamed of.

I know some days are extremely difficult, especially if you get a challenging group. We have all been there as teachers, but we always overcome and rise up for another day. Because if you are anything like me, you would "die if you cannot teach." This is the glory of being an educator as our calling, enabling our students to break free from ignorance while passing the torch of inner and outer knowledge.

You are the authority figure and leader in your classroom, and you can help prevent and respond to bullying in schools by using some of the guidelines provided in this manual. My hope is that by using the learning model and any of the class activities, you will be able to cultivate moments of empathy and compassion in your classroom.

To my inspirational educators: Jane Elliott and Jim Gavin, who modeled some of the greatest images of what a caring and dynamic teacher should be. And finally, Raju Ramanathan, my guru and meditation teacher, who taught me how to love unconditionally and to constantly feel gratitude from a state of breathing consciousness. To my dear friends, family, and editors, I thank you for your support throughout this journey.

Illustrated by Kevin Dunn

GLOBAL EDUCATIONAL HARMONY

When I was in high school at a private Catholic all-girls school, I observed and was part of many forms of bullying. As a bystander, bully, and victim, miserable in my classroom and uninterested in learning, I often would ponder, "What could make this high-school experience *better*?" The answer that always came to mind instinctively was for students to be able to get to know one another better by sitting together in a way that allowed eye contact to happen and one's true self to emerge and be shared without judgement. A setting where deep connections and honest feelings were shared allowing for real personal growth. Unfortunately, too many teachers do not have the time, desire, or energy for this type of "group sharing" and instead, use the traditional lecturing format, preventing students from connecting on a deeper level, thus allowing for the bullying and segregation to continue.

I learned the key to this secret in college and university, in my Race, Anthropology, and Racism courses, when I studied and viewed Jane Elliott's notorious Blue-Eyed Brown-Eyed exercise and documentary called "A Collar in My Pocket." After practically throwing a chair over each time, I soon realized, this is exactly what schools need to *Do*, not only *Show* on video or *Teach*. This exercise became the principles of my teaching to come, and the foundation of this teachers' manual, known as *experiential* learning strategies.

Jane Elliott's exercise was one of the most degrading, humbling, and transformational learning and teaching experiences I have ever had. I urge you to watch her documentaries, which are known internationally for their ethical procedure and unique way of teaching *empathy* in the classroom. Years later, I was taught first-hand by Mrs. Elliott, enabling me to continue our work and develop more tools that teachers can use in their classroom.

The Blue-Eyed Brown-Eyed exercise shed light on white privilege, bullying, sexism and all other *isms* we have in our society today, and shared the key to what I had hoped for in high school—a setting of openness, understanding and *empathy*.

Kenneth B. Clark, who was the first black president of the American Psychological Association and conducted the first Black & White Doll Experiment in the 1940s, noted: *"A major and inescapable goal of educational institutions is to broaden the perspective of human beings. To develop a truly functional empathy. To free human beings from the constrictions of ignorance, superstition, hostility and other forms of inhumanity. Jane Elliott's contribution, as described in William Peters' A Class Divided Then and Now demonstrates that it is possible to educate and produce a class of human beings united by understanding, acceptance and empathy."* (Peters. A Class Divided: Then and Now, 1987) Jane Elliott is an internationally known teacher, lecturer, diversity trainer and recipient of the National Mental Health Association Award for Excellence in Education. For additional information, visit www.janeelliott.com.

WHY EDUCATORS NEED THIS MANUAL

The Glory of Education's *Preventing Bullying: A Manual for Teachers in Promoting Global Educational Harmony* is a comprehensive guide for educators to gain insights, information, valuable resources and classroom- based student learning activities that are of great urgency and gravity in our societies today. It is important to note that there is no single cure or strategy that will stop or *end* bullying because each case is unique and should be treated accordingly.

But first, you must *believe* that your students can change, see them in this positive light, envision them in their most empathic and caring states, and maintain it long enough so that they *become it*. This is the greatest *gift* a teacher can ever give to their student—to believe in them and see their full potential as remarkable, compassionate, and beautiful children.

The problem is, teachers receive very little training on classroom management, bullying prevention or conflict resolution while achieving their bachelor's degree in education. Once they enter the classroom, educators report feeling stressed, unequipped, scared and sometimes even threatened by the bullies in their class. Hence, it is essential to put our "grown-up pants" on and take charge by using the activities and intervention strategies provided throughout this manual.

Teachers will not only create a positive learning environment, but also pave the way for their students' healthy emotional development. In this manual, teachers will learn how to set a positive tone in their classroom, build peer relationships, promote inclusivity, and make sure each student feels safe, valued, and able to learn in a stress-free environment.

In other words, each day that passes without our efforts in the prevention of bullying, is another day where students may feel:

- No motivation to learn.
- Anxiety when going to school.
- Loneliness and rejection by peers.
- Physical and/or emotional distress (sickness, stomach aches).

- Humiliation, anger and/or depression from being bullied.
- Trauma and/or shock associated with cyberbullying.
- Thoughts of revenge or even suicide.
- Feelings of regret and/or guilt carried into their adult lives.

A wise man once told me during my quest for a solution-based anti-bullying program:

> *"There is no need to teach anti-bullying, we must only teach pro-love and compassionate education."* — Raju Datta Yogi Raja

So how do we teach *pro-love* and compassionate education? As educators, we must be aware of the emotional repercussions of bullying and how easily it can be prevented in the comfort and safety of our classrooms. Although using preventative efforts involves a conscious effort and extra time on our parts, it will be appreciated by everyone in class. You have the power to promote compassionate education which will change the entire school environment. Let us begin to show you how to create this atmosphere with your own strength, knowledge, passion, and perseverance.

There is Hope

> *"Once you choose hope, anything is possible."* — Christopher Reeve

We all know that bullying is prevalent throughout the world. We see it on television, in politics, in sports, on social media and in global news. Therefore, we need community-wide efforts that encourage non-violent behaviors and promote harmony. Since schools are the most central place of learning, we must take responsibility for our students' academic and personal success by bringing opportunities for personal growth, understanding and healing to the classroom.

These activities will help students:

- Understand bullying and its effects.
- Share their unique stories.
- Learn empathy and compassion.

- Acknowledge their roles in bullying as well as their role in the prevention of it.
- Get to know their peers and build closer peer relationships.
- Gain assertiveness and leadership skills.
- Become advocates against all acts of bullying.

We have come a long way and it is important that we acknowledge how far we've progressed as a community in this fight against bullying:

- School policies have been modified and government bills passed.
- Police officials are instilling laws against assault and cyberbullying.
- National conferences about bullying and tackling solutions are being held.
- Media support and social recognition of bullying and its long-term impact is expanding.
- Non-profit organizations, such as WiredSafety.org and other social networking tools are growing in order to help support victims of cyber-bullying and harassment.
- Principals, teachers and counselors are becoming highly involved in bullying prevention and response techniques by offering student presentations and parent/teacher training and support.
- Several online resources can now be easily downloaded, printed and used for presentations, community events and classroom-based learning activities.
- Parents are becoming more involved and taking a stand to help protect the safety of their children in and outside of school.
- Students around the world are taking a stand and being trained on how to stand up for themselves and others against social, verbal, physical, cyber, racial, sexual and homophobic bullying.

The Ultimate Cure to Bullying

> *"If every eight-year-old in the world is taught meditation, we will eliminate violence from the world in one generation."* — Dalai Lama

Over the many years of personal, cultural, international and academic research on the topic of bullying, I found prominence in Thich Nhat Hanh's explanation of the root causes of abuse/bullying: *"When another person makes you suffer, it is because he suffers deeply within himself, and his suffering is spilling over. He does not need punishment; he needs help. That's the message he is sending."*

The ultimate cure to bullying is multi-dimensional and involves a community-wide effort in teaching students ethical and non-violent behaviors. Since bullying is a learned behavior, it can also be unlearned. Bullying prevention requires educating, protecting and empowering targets and bystanders; however, there is an underlying solution that many schools are catching onto that helps the inner well-being of the bullies in particular.

Currently, thousands of schools are implementing meditation and mindfulness practices such as deep breathing, moments of silence and positive incantations to start their day and before class periods for 5–10 minutes. Numerous studies have proven drastic and positive effects on students' level of happiness, academic performance, concentration, and depression and anxiety levels. Schools are also creating a peaceful space or meditation room where students who bully can go to reflect on their behavior and then discuss with counselors the logical consequences and ways to improve their behavior in the future.

Teachers can often relate to the saying, *"One bad apple can spoil the bunch,"* or one bad student can spoil the learning experience for the entire class. Therefore, the practice of meditation, deep breathing and/or mindfulness before the start of each class (or 2x per day) is the secret to bullying prevention in schools. Teaching acceptance of others and oneself will occur naturally when meditation and relaxation occur. Bullies who are suffering and overflowing with anger will, in due time, gain a new calm sense of self that will shift into being more open and caring individuals. In other words, if the aggressors or bullies were calm, balanced and truly happy inside, it would be impossible for them to bully others.

Here is a video clip from Oprah Winfrey's show on the most non-violent school in America using meditation: www.youtube.com/watch?v=1NEpzIMHQvg.

ABOUT THE AUTHORS

Christina Theophilos, M.Ed. & Founder of The Glory of Education

Christina Theophilos, M.Ed. is a university lecturer, yoga therapist, meditation instructor and educational consultant. She has done extensive research in behavioral psychology and contributed to the field of safe sexual education, anti-bullying and anti-discrimination by producing teacher's manuals, videos and other educational resources.

After having witnessed numerous cases of abuse and as a target of cyberbullying, she decided to devote herself to bringing peace and harmony across the globe through educational trainings and materials. Christina was drawn to South Korea, where she believed that her services were needed most, since South Korea has some of the highest numbers of suicide rates in the world. This led to the creation of *The Glory of Education*.

She is recognized for her empowering teachers training and student presentations across Canada and East Asia, which are based on the principles of Jane Elliott, the renowned anti-discrimination educator from the notorious "Blue-Eyed Brown-Eyed Exercise." After having reached thousands in her efforts to reduce the number of deaths caused by suicide, teen pregnancies and other at-risk youth behaviors, she now extends her solution-based strategies and classroom-based activities to the frontline of schools and communities. She is currently a lecturer at the University of Sherbrooke, where she provides teachers with crisis management, stress management and practical intervention strategies.

Christina often incorporates relaxation and meditation practices in her sessions, which she believes are the foundations for building a greater sense of peace, appreciation and acceptance of self and others. She believes that education can change the world if we unanimously cultivate moments of truth, hence realizing the glory of education.

Raju Ramanathan, M.Sc., Spiritual Mentor, Teacher, Author & Scientist

Mr. Raju Ramanathan, also known as Datta Yogi Raja, is a renowned scientist of both the inner and the outer worlds. At the age of 13, he started teaching meditation to his teachers and priests in his native village in India. While in college, he began teaching meditation, under the guidance of Swami Chinmayananda and Sivananda, to his fellow students in Engineering and in other temples and spiritual communities.

After completing his doctoral work in Space Sciences, Raju came to work for several major space contractors for NASA and continued sharing his passion for meditation to those in the corporate world. One of the corporations recognized Raju as their "teacher, mentor and guru with cherished friendships across many of their companies." For more than twenty years, Raju has been empowering individuals in Europe, Asia, the USA, and Canada. His unique approach brings life-transforming spiritual message to people of all religious paths and cultural backgrounds. All those who are concerned about the well-being of today's world will find Raju's teachings enlightening and inspirational.

Raju has spent the last 30 years teaching and coaching professionals in the art and science of relaxation using new ways of breathing and meditating with music in the advanced retreats that he conducts. Many participants have reported the healing effects of this approach.

Many psychiatrists and doctors have learnt advanced relaxation techniques. Recent lectures include the ones delivered to 100 doctors of the Indian Medical association in Chicago, 100 doctors of Southern Illinois School of Medicine in Springfield, IL, and the Psychology Department of University of Chicago, to name a few. He has also given talks to hundreds of doctors to create awareness of cures for chronic diseases, like cancer. Mr. Ramanathan is also a certified yoga teacher from "Yoga Bliss Institute" and trained by Dr. Madan Bali, who is recognized for his contributions to the field of complementary medicine.

Since the year 2015, Raju has been mentoring Christina Theophilos in the field of energy healing and spiritual psychology. He has also personally guided Christina in the process of developing teaching strategies for schools and universities, especially related to complex and current day crises such as addiction, depression, bullying and other forms of human suffering. Mindfulness and meditation have been the spiritual foundations of his teachings, which has impacted the development of solutions presented in Christina's work.

Raju's teachings center around the fact that human evolution must rise over and beyond Charles Darwin's thesis on the *Origin of Species*:

"The widespread notion that evolution happened because of the 'survival of fittest' ideology is wrong actually. Darwin himself pointed out towards the end of his thesis that further human evolution can only happen through sympathy, kindness, and compassion. This has been forgotten globally and my wish for teachers to develop and apply in the context of their classroom.

Current day issues in the classrooms, such as bullying, have resulted from this fundamental misunderstanding that aggression and competition are the only ways to succeed in life. Children should not be 'surviving.' They should be growing and blossoming into healthy and happy individuals. Problems such as bullying in schools will automatically disappear, thus giving rise to *Global Educational Harmony*." — Raju Ramanathan

To find out more about Mr. Datta Yogi Raja, please visit his website: www.rajuramanathan.com.

SECTION 1

BULLYING OVERVIEW

PREVENTING BULLYING:
A Manual For Teachers In Promoting Global Educational Harmony

WHAT IS BULLYING?

"When another person makes you suffer, it is because he suffers deeply within himself, and his suffering is spilling over. He does not need punishment; he needs help. That's the message he is sending." — Thich Nhat Hanh (Buddhist monk, Nobel Peace Prize winner)

Everyone can relate to bullying. Almost everyone has been a witness, target and bully at some point of their lives. This is the reason why this topic is so intriguing to thousands of people across the globe who are in search of healing and solutions to creating Global Educational and Societal Harmony.

According to literature, bullying occurs when someone repeatedly and purposefully says or does something harmful or abusive to another person who has *less power* than them either physically, psychologically, financially or politically. Bullying is about the use and misuse of one's *power* over another individual in one context or another. This imbalance of power is seen throughout human history and is one of the root causes of our "bullying and uncivilized" recurring behaviors. It has been passed on from generation to generation, leaving children with emotional scars and confusing experiences that make them helpless, uncertain and lost in their pure potential of being caring individuals.

Bullying is seen *everywhere,* from the moment we turn on our televisions to the so-called leaders running our countries, administrators at our schools, sports coaches, parents and peers. Bullying is also experienced in the classroom, which is a microcosm of our society, and teachers often subconsciously allow it to happen. Therefore, to create a world of young adults, we must begin teaching in a different way and address the issues that are most meaningful to them. Once this occurs, learning can be done in a state of calm and safety.

Commonly seen imbalances of power include:

- *Economic*, when the bully has more money than the target.
- *Physical*, based on relative size or height or on the number of friends they have in their peer group, which acts as a social army.
- *Social*, belonging to a group of popular kids or jocks, which brings them up the social ladder).
- *Identity*, including ethnicity, skin color, and gender or sexual orientation viewed as different from the dominant group.
- *Intellectual*, expressed as "I know more than you, I am smarter than you, and therefore I'm superior."
- *Age*, if older kids feel they have more authority over kids in younger grades.
- *Online*, if the bully is anonymous or has wide influence within the target's social group.

The key elements of bullying are:

- The imbalance of power between the bully and the target.
- The bully's intent to do harm, whether bodily, emotionally, socially, or sexually.
- The target's suffering.
- Repetition over time (Pepler and Craig, 1999).

Bullying can be **direct**, when the bully confronts the target face-to-face; or **indirect**, when the bully attacks the target's reputation when the target is not around. Examples of indirect bullying include, but are not limited to: spreading rumors, gossiping, writing insulting graffiti about the target, threats made by email or text messages and ostracizing the target.

PREVENTING BULLYING:
A Manual For Teachers In Promoting Global Educational Harmony

Five Types of Bullying

The five most common types of bullying behavior include cyber, sexual, verbal, emotional (nonverbal) and physical. Often, people bully to control, exclude, embarrass or feel superior to the target. Bullying is often homophobic, sexist, racist and/or is directed towards people who are overweight, have disabilities, or have intellectual gifts that make them stand out. Below are the five types of bullying and some examples for each:

1. **Cyber**	<ul><li>sending malicious rumors or gossiping</li><li>posting humiliating pictures or videos using social media</li><li>sending threats or insults about a person's character, appearance or behavior</li></ul>
2. **Sexual**	<ul><li>intimidation and unhealthy relationships that may involve verbal and physical abuse</li><li>sexual harassment, rumors, gossip, looks, gestures or groping</li><li>rape</li><li>making negative remarks towards LGBTQ individuals</li><li>"sexting" by sharing intimate photos or videos of the target</li></ul>
3. **Verbal**	<ul><li>name-calling, sometimes cloaked as "teasing"</li><li>harassing targets to do or say something</li><li>spreading gossip, lies or rumors</li><li>insulting someone's family, status or religion</li><li>yelling at someone</li><li>insulting or nagging</li><li>making verbal threats or demands</li><li>making noises as the bullied person passes by</li><li>jokes that demean religions, races, sexual orientations or disabilities</li><li>death threats</li></ul>

4. **Physical**
   - threatening postures such as making a fist or cornering someone
   - stealing ("jacking") the target's lunch, money, clothing, homework or books
   - pushing, punching, pulling hair, flicking or bumping into the target on purpose
   - use or showing of weapons, such as a knife, blunt instruments or a gun
   - throwing, hiding or damaging a person's belongings
   - spitting or flicking paper, rubber bands or any other object at the person
   - burping in the target's face
   - pressuring the person to smoke, drink, steal or engage in potentially harmful or criminal activities

5. **Emotional (Nonverbal)**
   - intentional exclusion from groups, games, sports, conversations, planned activities or parties
   - ignoring the person or giving them the "silent treatment"
   - whispering and pointing while looking at the target
   - glaring ("dirty looks")
   - sticking out the tongue at the target
   - intimidating or threatening gestures

Factors Contributing to Bullying

> *"We are the sum-total of our experiences. Those experiences, be they positive or negative, make us the person we are, at any given point in our lives. And, like a flowing river, those same experiences, and those yet to come, continue to influence and reshape the person we are, and the person we become. None of us are the same as we were yesterday, nor will be tomorrow."* — B. J. Neblett

The age-old question of nature versus nurture is interesting when considering the root cause of bullying. One's "nature" boils down to the instinctive choices one makes in the present moment based on our natural tendencies or learned from our environment. Bullying tendencies and influences generally fall into five categories: individual, brain development, family, peers or community.

Individual

Bullying may be associated with characteristics such as temperament, attention problems, or hyperactivity, all of which can easily increase the risk of aggressive behaviors. At other times, a bully may simply be in an egocentric state, concerned only about his or her personal pleasure, using intimidation and control to cover his own insecurities and inadequacies. When it comes to bullying, every situation is different. Causes and motivations underlying bullying may include neglect at home, socioeconomic issues, mental health issues, or rejection by peers, but what remains consistent is the predominance of bullying during adolescence.

Brain Development

An important factor to consider in trying to prevent bullying is brain development during adolescence. Since the frontal cortex of the brain is not fully developed until the mid-twenties, adolescents are less capable of making logical judgments and more likely to be controlled by impulses and emotions. One area that is fully developed, however, is the *nucleus accumbens*, a section of the brain that seeks pleasure, acceptance, and reward. For example, a student who bullies may experience feelings of superiority and false confidence, especially if encouraged by peers. As a result, teens often engage in stereotypical, thrill-seeking and sometimes at- risk behaviors such as peer abuse, bullying and intimidation, or unprotected sex without regarding the potentially negative outcomes of their actions.

The good news is that during adolescence, the brain is like a sponge, always absorbing new ways of thinking and behaving. This phenomenon, known as *plasticity*, gives hope to teachers who believe in the importance of educating and empowering students to make sound decisions. Students are capable of learning that joking around, using sarcasm towards a person, or excluding someone because they are different is hurtful and a form of bullying.

Family

The family can be a strong contributing factor to bullying. Children learn all sorts of behaviors from their parents, siblings and relatives. Bullying tendencies can result from children modeling what they have witnessed or experienced firsthand. Family upbringing often helps determine whether children have been taught right from wrong, civilized behavior and empathy towards others. Family-related stresses such as divorce, aggression within the home, single parenting or ineffective parenting are important variables to take into account when attempting to understand acting out or frustrated behavior.

Peers

Research shows that bullies may be perceived as popular students who have many friends, high status and high self-esteem, and are often considered "cool" among their peers. Bystanders can unwittingly become bullies by succumbing to peer pressure and mimicking the abusive behaviors of the "cool crowd." Students, especially during adolescence, have a need to fit in, and this need may transform them into seemingly uncaring monsters who bully one another without a clear understanding of the impact of their behavior.

Community

Bullying is a learned behavior that the aggressor becomes exposed to in their surrounding environment or community. Societal norms play a part in how negative behavior is propagated throughout pop culture, which glorifies conflict and competition, highlighting the gap between those who are perceived as inferior and superior. Unless we model and reinforce a standard of understanding, equality and non-violent behavior, bullying will continue. Positive role models and open dialogues about these issues are crucial for students at this stage to enable them to develop a healthy perspective and appropriate behavior.

Bullying from a Lifespan Perspective

Bullying in all its forms is often seen as a serious social problem that affects so many people's lives. What is notable about bullying is that if it stems in early on in childhood, it can often continue and/or repeat itself in adulthood. Some behavioral theorists believe that if a child does not mature or grow out of this aggressive pattern, they will continuously crave the need for power and control over others in later stages in their lives. In the most serious cases, if abusive behaviors are not dealt with during childhood, they may escalate into more serious criminal acts, including gang involvement, date violence, marital abuse and child or elder abuse. Therefore, the earlier we intervene in schools and in our homes, the better it will be for everyone as a global society.

Table 1.0. Developmental Patterns of Bullying: Power and Aggression

Normative Aggression	CHILDHOOD
Bullying	
Sexual Harassment	
Delinquency	
Gang Involvement	ADOLESCENCE
Date Violence	
Workplace Harassment	
Marital Abuse	ADULTHOOD
Child Abuse	
Elderly Abuse	

Where Bullying Occurs

Bullying usually begins in elementary school and escalates during adolescence and can continue into adult life. It generally becomes most prominent and detrimental during middle and high school, when sadly it contributes to so many teen suicides.

Unfortunately, various forms of bullying occur in most schools across the globe. Bullying is often maintained in social settings such as the classroom, playground and home, and now, with the advent of social media, is ever-present online.

Teachers, staff and parents often do not realize when or where bullying is occurring, since it typically happens in the absence of immediate adult supervision. Bullying usually takes place outside of the classroom, in bathrooms, hallways, during lunch hour or after school, when the target is vulnerable and often when an audience is present.

Cyberbullying

The two most common types of bullying associated with modern technology are cyberbullying and sexting, which differ from traditional bullying in that the bullies get to hide behind cell phones and screen names. The bully cannot see the person face-to-face, and this anonymity makes it easier to do harm. Nonetheless, these forms of bullying, both relentless and persistent, involve a need for power over the person on the opposite end.

Students who grow up immersed in technology are now called "digital natives" and it has become part of their competitive nature to put others down using social media in order to feel superior, popular or to joke around, without realizing the negative repercussions of their actions. Students need to be taught boundaries such as privacy settings: where to draw the line, whom to trust and what qualifies as online harassment and abuse. Cyberbullying can cause serious emotional harm and trauma to the person being targeted—in some cases, detrimental enough to cause thoughts of suicide or even steps toward committing the act. Students who are targets of cyberbullying need to know how to identify a criminal act online, and how or where to report incidents. Cyberbullying includes the online dissemination of unfair rumors, modified photographs, and humiliating photographs or videos, including assaults or beatings.

While it is becoming quite a common practice amongst teens to "sext," meaning to send graphic images and messages via their mobile devices, it is important for students to know that there are legal consequences for such actions. For example, people (including minors) who share or distribute sexually explicit images or messages can be charged with *making or distributing child pornography* or be accused of *sexual harassment*, depending on your county's criminal codes. It is important that students learn the risks involved in exposing themselves online and learn not to ask for photos and never to release them, or they can be charged with creating, possessing and distributing child pornography.

The punishments for these actions can be as harsh as incarceration and staying on their criminal record for a lifetime. Therefore, students must be taught not to take, or force others to take, sexual images or videos of themselves or others, and most importantly, not share or post such images or messages if they happen to come across them. If students receive such images or messages, then it is important that they learn to take quick action and prevent the perpetrator from sending more by reporting the abuse immediately to the proper authorities.

Encourage students to talk to their parents, school counselor, or the police if they are involved in sexting. Examples of sexting can include sending, posting, receiving, forwarding and sharing sexually explicit messages, images or videos (of oneself or others) to someone else via a mobile device or email. It can also encompass situations such as couples sharing photos between each other, individuals sharing pictures of themselves in hopes of attracting another person and sharing pictures of someone else without their consent.

Bystanders

"Fear is deeply rooted within our genes. Whenever there is more than one person, there is fear. This is our teaching. If you are fearless then you are full of love." — The Yogic Way, Swami G

Bystanders are people who witness bullying occur, are aware that they aren't doing anything to help the target, and often sympathize with them. Like most people's instinctive fear of being ostracized from the majority group, bystanders do not want to "get involved," be at the center of attention, lose popularity or be the next target. Unfortunately, bystanders are highly influenced by their peers' behavior, that they neglect their own moral obligations and values of supporting the target in need.

As educators, we must teach bystanders assertiveness and resolution skills and help build their confidence, to where they become fearless and part of the solution.

Children at Risk

Characteristics of people who are targets of bullying vary according to every individual situation and social environment. Simply put, targets are people of all ages who have had the misfortune of encountering a bully. Call it bad luck, poor timing, or fate; anybody can become a target of bullying.

Research shows, however, that both genetics and one's individual character of being socially withdrawn, introverted, or exceptional to the group can increase the likelihood of a predisposition to the role of target. For example, targets are usually considered "atypical" because of the way they dress, walk and talk, or their physical or mental differences or disabilities. Targets can also be bullied due to their sexual orientation, ethnicity or socioeconomic status.

Family stress can also play a role in shaping a target's odd behavior that can lead to rejection by their peers, isolation and loss of reputation. Overprotective parents who "shelter" their child from outside socialization can cause their child to have a lack of social engagement skills or assertiveness. The lack of assertiveness, having many friends, or being shy and vulnerable are common factors that most targets have, which the bully can unconsciously pick up on, knowing that his or her chances of retribution are slim to none.

Some common reasons why targets often do not speak up or assert themselves include:

- Fear that the bullying occurrences will escalate.
- The lack of support in their current environment.
- A belief that their parents, the police, counselors or teachers can't do anything or a fear that the same elders will declare them to be wrong or overreacting.
- A feeling of helplessness.
- Their hope that ignoring the problem will eventually make it stop.

Every so often, not becoming a target of bullying depends on whether the individual has high self-confidence, self-acceptance social skills, and a few close friends and the quality and strength of those friendships. Identifying who is at risk of or vulnerable to bullying should not be our main concern as educators. Instead, we must address a bully's lack of empathy and insensitivity towards others.

It is important, however, to remind those who are targets that they have certain characteristics that the bully subconsciously sees as threatening, desirable or simply "too good" to speak up for themselves. The bully's actions are used to cover their underlying pain, anger and/or insecurities. The bully literally uses the target (i.e., punching bag) to deflect their painful emotions, knowing the target will not confront them. This need for power or dominance over others is something the target must realize, and in turn, they must speak up and assert themselves in any way possible until the bullying stops, and it will if they follow these steps with pride and conviction.

Bullying Outcomes

> *"Bullying builds character like nuclear waste creates superheroes. It's a rare occurrence and often does much more damage than endowment"* – Zack W. Van

The results of bullying are significant and should not be taken lightly. The effects go far deeper than what meets the eye. Reducing bullying to just a phase that every child goes through, or a learning experience that will make them stronger, overlooks its true severity and the effect it can have on the bullied person. Bullying is much more crippling than we think, and it has grown worse over the years since the advent of social media. The results of bullying often involve a "ripple effect" and can be detrimental to all areas of one's life, including emotional, cognitive, physical and social.

The four possible outcomes of bullying are:

1. Emotional
2. Intellectual
3. Physical
4. Social

<u>Emotional:</u>

- Targets are usually shocked and surprised at first by the abuse, but then, fear paralyzes them.
- Targets may have a sickening fear; they may feel like their world is unsafe from people who are superior to them and dread going to school each day. Anxiety consumes them.
- Learned helplessness sets in, which is the belief that there is nothing they can do to escape or help make their situation better.
- They become depressed and angry towards people that they feel comfortable with, like their parents.

- They feel undesirable and incapable of handling the situation and "hit rock bottom" as they cannot bear the distress, and hence usually find solutions or seek help.
- Identity crisis occurs when targets forget who they really are and lose their sense of self-worth. Self-loathing and believing what the bully may perceive them as is what they begin to identify with. The "Looking Glass Theory" by Charles Cooley helps us understand this concept by having the people in our close environment serve as "mirrors" that reflect images of ourselves. In other words, people and targets of bullying can often shape their self-concept based on their understanding of how others perceive them.

There are three main components to this theory:

1. We imagine how we must appear to others.
2. We imagine and react to what we feel their judgment of that appearance must be.
3. We develop ourselves through the judgments of others.

Intellectual:

- Reduced concentration, memory difficulties in and outside of class and incomplete homework or assignments.
- So-called "disaster movies" of the worst-case scenarios and future encounters replay themselves in their minds, sometimes including fantasizing revenge.
- Gifted or intelligent students may hide their potential and knowledge for fear of being ridiculed, thus negatively impacting their achievements and talents.
- Students who are academically challenged may hide their disabilities or difficulties and fear being labeled as "stupid" or outcasts.

- Targets often do not contribute or ask questions during class in order to avoid attention. This can result in low academic performance, high school dropouts and discontinuation of further education.
- The person may be plagued by thoughts of revenge, helplessness and suicide.

Physical:

- Bruises, scratches, cuts and other wounds caused by bullies' physical violence
- Headaches, backaches, stomach aches, bedwetting, loss of hair, skin disorders, sleep difficulties, nightmares, irregular menstruation, loss of appetite or overeating, pale skin, tension and a weak immune system, all of which can result in stress-related illnesses
- Smoking, drug and substance abuse, absenteeism, changing schools, dropping out of high school, cutting and even suicide

Social:

- Targets of bullying may often avoid and feel uncomfortable, tense, and insecure around their peers (who perhaps remind them of their vulnerability).
- Friends distance themselves from the target and merge with new friends, fearing being associated with the target or getting bullied themselves.
- Targets may be attached to one friend to feel secure and not alone. Also, they may remain in a "trendy or secure" group of friends where they are being bullied, as they would rather feel a sense of belonging to that group than be considered an "outcast."
- Parents often feel helpless and inexperienced on how to help and support their children. The child may isolate themselves from family members and avoid burdening or disappointing their parents.

- Targets may avoid areas where they can be potentially victimized, such as large crowds, school buses or the cafeteria, where supervision is less noticed. As a result of their exclusion and disassociation, they are often not invited to parties, are last to join games or group projects and have a poor social life.
- Targets may become isolated and fear being hurt and rejected again, so they often have difficulty making new friends, gaining social skills and trusting others.

PREVENTING BULLYING:
A Manual For Teachers In Promoting Global Educational Harmony

Long-Term Effects of Bullying

*"Sticks and stones may break my bones, **and words will cut me deeply.**"*

Problems caused by all forms of abuse will not necessarily cease when the bullying stops. Research shows that when the trauma of any sort occurs, there is a shift in our cells that may result in serious repercussions for our entire human state and system. Therefore, targets of bullying may need long-term support. Studies show that victims of abuse and bullying may:

- Become a bully at an older age (from all the repressed anger) and use violence or aggression to resolve conflict.
- Have a damaged self-concept and identity.
- Continue to be a target at a later age (i.e., at the workplace).
- Experience difficulty in making and trusting new friends.
- Have difficulty building or maintaining romantic relationships.
- Tend to fall behind in their studies, at times resulting in school dropouts.
- Have their career and dreams jeopardized as a result of non-completion of their education.
- Hold tension or bitterness with an aspect of their life that has been criticized, yet is unalterable (such as their sexual orientation, minority group membership, religious affiliation, etc.).
- Develop eating disorders (e.g., excessive eating, anorexia, bulimia, or using steroids) in order to gain some sort of control or comfort in their lives.
- Become promiscuous and unsafe in their sexual behaviors, lacking self-respect.
- Experiment with or become addicted to cigarettes, drugs or alcohol to cope with their stress.
- Contemplate, attempt, and in some cases even commit suicide.

The prevention and response to bullying are possible via education, intervention, support, counseling and proper guidance. As educators, the responsibility is on us to stay alert and identify possible targets of bullying, as well as perpetrators. We simply need to take the time to help support victims of bullying by helping them find their inner and outer strength to overcome the given situation.

SECTION 2

HOW SCHOOLS CAN HELP PREVENT BULLYING

"Education can change the world." – Nelson Mandela

PREVENTING BULLYING:
A Manual For Teachers In Promoting Global Educational Harmony

We are grateful to live in a privileged and educated society that cares about the wellbeing of our youth. Bullying has shattered too many lives and together we have come to realize that enough is enough, and the time to act for the prevention of bullying is now. Through proper education and support, we can make our schools a safe and respectful learning environment.

The commitment to bullying prevention and response must be across the board—students, teachers, parents, administrators and the community must all come together in this effort. Often, parents and students report not feeling supported by their school administration, while teachers also report a sense of helplessness and not knowing what the appropriate measures should be.

The impact of this, unfortunately, is on our students, who are left feeling depressed, harassed, alone and, in some cases, suicidal. In order to encourage and instill confidence in our students that they can stand up against bullying, schools must send out a strong message emphasizing their non-tolerance towards any form of bullying and their commitment towards its eradication through education.

Challenges Schools Face in Preventing Bullying

Despite all our efforts in trying to reduce or even eliminate bullying, our endeavor isn't over. Bullying remains a nightmare for schools to handle, especially after their students have engaged in cyberbullying, which can now be considered an offense of the perpetrators for "distributing" child pornography. Nevertheless, there are several social problems that we still need to overcome:

Problem #1: *Some schools do not have an action plan on how to:*

1. Implement preventative school measures and policies.
2. Create open lines of communication among teachers, parents and staff members.
3. Manage and follow up on bullying incidents.
4. Discipline or effectively teach bullies (offenders).

Problem #2: *Some schools lack government support and funding for:*

1. Training of teachers and staff on how to prevent or respond to bullying.
2. Bullying prevention specialists or guest speakers.
3. Educational tools, materials or resources.

Problem #3: *Teachers are unable to handle a bullying situation. Reasons for this include:*

1. Not knowing *how* to intervene. They are ill-equipped due to lack of training and resources.
2. Lack of administrative support.
3. Feeling that it is not their responsibility, so they choose to stay uninvolved.
4. Lack of time to address the problem while teaching their curriculum.

5. Having too many students, with too many problems, and feeling overwhelmed.
6. Sometimes feeling afraid of, and/or intimidated by, the bully.
7. Believing that bullying is a part of adolescence and requires no adult or school intervention.

Problem #4: *The legal system is lagging in the advancement and misuse of online technology. Some of the imposing factors include:*

1. Allotting time to identify the problem (e.g., cyberbullying) as a criminal act and where to draw the line.
2. Creating new laws under the umbrella term for violence and abuse from and against minors.
3. Training law enforcement personnel on how to apply and enforce the new law(s) for the specific district or territory.

Problem #5: *The term "BULLYING" has been exploited. Reasons being:*

1. The term has been overused, losing its impact and importance.
2. Students do not associate themselves with the term as they have become desensitized to it.

Questions to Consider About Your School's Anti-Bullying Initiatives

Schools across the globe are coming together to bring about change, collaboration, and safety in their educational curriculums. Questions remain, however, for educators and school administration to consider in their efforts in preventing bullying:

1. Is there an anti-bullying action plan in place at your school?
2. What is your school's code of acceptable behaviors and the sanctions against all forms of bullying (i.e., physical, cyber, sexual or verbal)?
3. Are the codes of conduct and sanctions well known by all students?
4. Is there a committee that handles concerns and questions about bullying for parents, teachers and students?
5. Are there seminars and workshops offered to parents, teachers, and students on ways to prevent bullying?
6. Are there follow-up or re-assessment procedures in place to ensure that the most effective prevention efforts are made?
7. Are students educated about bullying and encouraged to report all forms of abuse?

PREVENTING BULLYING:
A Manual For Teachers In Promoting Global Educational Harmony

Seven Steps to Developing Your School's Action Plan

"Our school acts as a microcosm of society, making the classroom the best place to learn about bullying." — Christina Theophilos

The following are seven simple steps on how schools can support the efforts towards bullying prevention:

Step 1: Develop an ACTION PLAN in collaboration with administrators, teachers and parents to set acceptable CODES OF BEHAVIOR and SANCTIONS. (Copy and distribute "Understanding Your School's Conduct of Behavior Form.")

Step 2: Develop COMMUNICATION STRATEGIES to disseminate code and SANCTIONS to all students. For example, using posters, flyers, school assemblies, parent/student contract agreements and so on. (Copy and distribute "Understanding Our School's Sanctions Form" provided.)

Step 3: Appoint a COMMITTEE for parents, teachers and students to contact about their questions or concerns.

Step 4: Schedule REGULAR MEETINGS or workshops with staff and parents to assess the effectiveness of the ACTION PLAN and modify and update codes and sanctions as required.

Step 5: Develop a student forum or distribute the BULLYING ASSESSMENT QUESTIONNAIRE (provided) to assess student reaction, acceptance and the effectiveness of the action plan, and incorporate their suggestions to involve them in the process.

Step 6: Schedule SEMINARS, workshops and training for parents, teachers and students to heighten their awareness and provide up-to-date strategies and skills to prevent bullying. (See tips for teachers on preventing bullying in the classroom.)

Step 7: Have follow-up meetings with school staff to reassess the effectiveness of the ACTION PLAN.

> *Lack of intervention implies that bullying is acceptable and can be performed without fear of consequences. If there are punishments, the responsibility is diffused among peers.*
>
> — Pepler & Craig, 1988

PREVENTING BULLYING:
A Manual For Teachers In Promoting Global Educational Harmony

How to Promote a Bully-Free School Environment

1. Train teachers, staff, and administrators on how to R*ecognize*, R*eact* and R*esolve* the bullying in school.
2. Encourage teachers to report bullying or misconduct using the "Heads Up" Form provided.
3. Have teachers integrate and choose bullying prevention or response activity (from this manual) that they feel comfortable facilitating in their classroom (at least once every few months).
4. Make sure all students have read and understood your school's policy for the proper conduct of behavior and the sanctions that could be applied, should they be broken.
5. Check-in with your students and find out if their needs are met by distributing the "Bullying Assessment Questionnaire."
6. Hang encouraging posters around your school promoting respect, friendship and non-violence.
7. Provide students with a bullying helpline number, either on the school's web page, via posters or distributed flyers. Create a confidential "bullying box" in the library or near the counselor or principal's office where students can insert their written stories or seek guidance. Support students in reporting and discussing bullying incidents with counselors, parents or police officers.
8. Have students advocate against bullying by wearing t-shirts, pins or hats that raise awareness about bullying. Let them form a Bullying Police Squad, student presentations, contests and so on, making sure everyone in the school feels safe, happy and able to learn.
9. Offer non-competitive in/after school activities such as dance, singing, aerobics or yoga to build better social experiences and skills.
10. Invite guest speakers and police officers, or show video clips of famous pop stars, sports icons or actors sharing stories about bullying and acts of kindness during student assemblies.

Bullying Prevention Objectives

In order to help prevent bullying, teachers should collaborate with their colleagues and administration to properly divide tasks and learning goals using the classroom-based activities provided that appeals to them and that they feel comfortable teaching. This way, students will gain information from all angles, having all their teachers support the fact that bullying will not be tolerated and knowing how to respond if a bullying situation occurs. Remember, knowledge is power, so presenting them with tools on how to respond while having an open forum to discuss their thoughts, feelings, and experiences will greatly benefit and transform them.

The most important element here is for teachers to work as a team, share a vision, and discuss *when* they will use the activities in order to balance out the topics throughout the school year.

Example: *Bullying Prevention Activities Divided – For Secondary 2 Teachers*

Month	Secondary 2 Teachers	Activities
September	Dave (History)	
	Mary (Science)	
	Amal (Ethics)	
October	Julie (Phys Ed)	
	Ted (English)	
	Nick (Math)	
November	Julie (Phys Ed)	
	Ted (English)	
	Nick (Math)	
December	Julie (Phys Ed)	
	Ted (English)	
	Julie (Phys Ed)	

PREVENTING BULLYING:
A Manual For Teachers In Promoting Global Educational Harmony

January	Ted (English)	
	Julie (Phys Ed)	
	Ted (English)	
February	Julie (Phys Ed)	
	Ted (English)	
	Julie (Phys Ed)	
March	Ted (English)	
	Julie (Phys Ed)	
	Ted (English)	
April	Julie (Phys Ed)	
	Ted (English)	
	Ted (English)	
May	Julie (Phys Ed)	
	Ted (English)	
	Julie (Phys Ed)	
June	Ted (English)	
	Julie (Phys Ed)	
	Ted (English)	

By sharing these insights and classroom-based learning activities, we hope to lower the occurrences of:

- Bullying, social rejection, gossiping.
- Low self-esteem, cutting (i.e., self-mutilation).
- Poor academic achievements.
- At-risk behaviors (i.e., unprotected sex, drugs and alcohol abuse).
- Depression, thoughts of suicide, or revenge.
- Discrimination, segregation.
- Ethnocentrism, prejudice.
- Homophobia, racist jokes.
- Stereotyping, white privilege.
- Eating disorders.
- Absenteeism.

Bullying Assessment Questionnaire

Your answers are anonymous and confidential in order to help STOP bullying.

1. How old are you? _____

2. Are you male or female? Please circle: MALE or FEMALE

3. What has your school done to help prevent bullying?

4. What do you think your school could do to help prevent and respond to bullying?

5. Have YOU ever:

    a. Witnessed bullying at your school? Circle: YES or NO

    b. Been a target of bullying? Circle: YES or NO

    c. If you answered "Yes" above, what type(s) of bullying was experienced?

    Circle: Verbal   Physical   Emotional   Online (Cyber)

6. What are some things teachers can do to stop bullying?

7. Would you like to share a bullying incident that you have witnessed or are involved in?

PREVENTING BULLYING:
A Manual For Teachers In Promoting Global Educational Harmony

Our School's Code of Conduct Form

ALL BULLYING INCIDENTS MUST BE REPORTED

BULLYING TYPES	I_____(your name) declare and promise not to:
CYBER	1. Send or display offensive text messages, emails or pictures. 2. Share sexual images of myself or others which is considered a criminal act and a form of child pornography. 3. Visually record, take pictures and share them with others if they are embarrassing or humiliating. 4. Harass, insult or use foul language using any form of social media. 5. Spread malicious rumor or gossip online. 6. Send threats or insult someone's character, appearance or behavior using any online media. 7. Damage computers, computer systems or computer networks on school grounds. 8. Use others' passwords or accounts. 9. Hack into others' accounts or personal folders.
SEXUAL	1. Make vulgar sexual comments towards others. 2. Attack someone in a sexual manner. 3. Touch someone (groping) in a sexual manner. 4. Stare/gesture at someone in a sexual manner. 5. Spread rumors about someone's sexual behavior or identity.
VERBAL	1. Interrupt when someone else is speaking. 2. Gossip about others or spread rumors that may jeopardize their image or integrity.

	3. Call people offensive names. 4. Speak offensively about a certain race, culture or religion. 5. Share a racist, culturally biased or offensive joke. 6. Use homophobic language such as "That's so gay." 7. Use sarcasm that insults or belittles someone. 8. Embarrass someone by teasing them (this is still considered bullying). 9. Scream or yell at someone. 10. Make verbal threats or demands.
PHYSICAL	1. Push, shove, punch, corner, pull hair or pinch anyone. 2. Steal or take anything that does not belong to me. 3. Destroy anything that isn't mine. 4. Use of or showing of any harmful objects/ weapons (knives, guns, etc.). 5. Any form of peer pressure to intimidate someone into "fitting in" (e.g., smoking, drinking, doing drugs, etc.).
EMOTIONAL	1. Ignore people when they are speaking. 2. Intentionally exclude my peers from activities or team sports. 3. Give dirty looks (i.e., eye-rolling when someone is speaking). 4. Stare, point or smirk at someone I do not like.

I _____ (**Print Your Name**) have read and understood our school's guidelines and will see that I follow these rules in order to help prevent any harm to myself or my fellow peers.

Student Signature: _____   Date: _____

Sanctions for Misconduct Form

BULLYING IS NOT TOLERATED. NO EXCEPTIONS OR EXCUSES.

<u>Sanctions for Misconduct & Abusive Behavior:</u>

1. Documentation of the bullying incident to school authorities.
2. A meeting with the principal and/or counselor with the persons involved in the bullying incident.
3. A meeting with all parents involved.
4. Logical consequences held for the abuser including:
   - A letter of apology to the target (1) summarizing the event, (2) explaining the reasons and outcomes of their actions and (3) how they will rectify the situation, and (4) what they have learned from this experience.
   - Assigned community work (i.e., homeless shelters, cleaning the school, no recess, detention) for the perpetrator to develop a deeper connection with their community and with others.
5. For severe cases or repeated acts of bullying, more appropriate remediation will be applied, including:
   - after school and lunch detentions.
   - counseling with proper authorities.
   - contact with police and law enforcement personnel.
   - prohibition to participate in school activities, trips, or sports events.
   - family intervention and therapy.
   - expulsion from school.

The sanctions will be aligned with the severity of the bullying misbehavior.

I _____ (**Print Your Name**) have read and understood our school's guidelines and will see that I follow these rules in order to help prevent any harm to my fellow peers.

Student Signature: _____ Date: _____

Giving Advice to Parents About Bullying

> *"The schools don't care. We have had so many interviews with principals and superintendents and they give you the same plastic smile ... and say, 'Yes, I understand, and I'll do everything I can,' and nothing is ever done. They say that kids will be kids, girls will be girls, and boys will be boys."*—
> Parent's statement from the documentary film Bully

As educators, we often find ourselves interacting with troubled and concerned parents whose child may be involved in a bullying situation. Therefore, it is important to get parents involved and ensure that they are prepared to handle the situation.

There are several steps one can take as a parent once a bullying situation has occurred. However, one must keep in mind that there are preventative measures that can be employed to avoid a bullying situation in the first place. Some of these include:

1. **Frequent communication with their child** about his/her activities and relationships at school. This will show the child that their parents are interested in learning about their day-to-day experiences, challenges and interactions.
2. **Providing positive feedback** when they have demonstrated courage in standing up against or preventing any potentially harmful situation.
3. **Reinforcing non-violence** and encouraging their child to think of solutions to problems in a manner that doesn't cause hurt or damage to another person. At this point, it is also important for parents to reserve their own opinions and emotions in front of their child and approach the situation in a calm manner. This will ensure that the child is not in an agitated or over-emotional state when discussing the situation.
4. **Listening to what their child has to say.** If the child gets the sense that parents do not think of their problems as "real" or don't

take their emotions seriously, they may feel embarrassed about bringing up issues and may not reach out to their parents for help or play down the situation.

5. **Familiarizing students with the school's anti-bullying policy and sanctions.** If available, parents should spend some time with their child reviewing the school's policy and sanctions on bullying so that they know what defines bullying and the possible repercussions associated.

6. **Collaborating with the school's administrators and staff** to discuss how their child is doing in school from an academic perspective but also in relation to their social interactions. This will give parents a heads up in case there are any early warning signs.

7. **Helping document bullying incidents.** For parents whose child is different, keeping documentation of incidents can help in providing a clear picture to the school administrators and authorities. Keeping a journal, along with photos of any physical abuse that may have taken place, is very beneficial.

8. **Seeking assistance from other parents in similar situations** where their child is a target or bully gives parents a sense that they are not alone, while also sharing parenting tips.

9. **Monitoring closely and not allowing bullying to dominate lives** encourage children to talk to their parents if any bullying situation recurs in the future. Parents should also stay vigilant, looking out for warning signs and constantly communicating with their child. For the targets of bullying, parents can help them build confidence and the necessary skills to face their environment. Enrolling these students in some classes (self-defense or any other skill-building classes) can help them make new friends and find a community in which they feel they belong.

Bullying Prevention Letter to Parents

Dear Parent / Guardian,

Laws define bullying as *"any repeated overt acts by a student or group of students directed against another student with the intent to ridicule, humiliate, harass or intimidate the other while on school grounds (including transportation vehicles and online) or at school-sponsored activities."*

Bullying is a serious issue, especially during adolescence, so our school is taking the initiative to enforce a zero-tolerance policy and collaborate with parents/guardians to ensure students' safety and overall well-being. Preventing bullying is most effectively understood when the message is conveyed from various channels: the classroom, at home and among peer groups. Therefore, our staff is giving special attention to this matter by encouraging teachers to discuss bullying using classroom-based learning activities and discussions.

In order to successfully convey the harmful effects of bullying, we encourage all parents/guardians to continue the discussion and make sure your child is behaving kindly towards others and getting the proper treatment from other peers at school, which will only enhance their learning and school experience.

If your child has witnessed or been a target of any form of abuse at school, please report it to your child's teacher, counselor, or administrator. It is important that students are encouraged to speak up for themselves and protected, without fear of retaliation. Let us continue to work together and create the best learning environment for your child.

Sincerely,

School Principal:
Contact information:
Email:
Contact number:

Important Signs of Bullying That Parents Should Know

Parents can choose to deal with bullying situations in several ways. Some decide to ignore the situation (thinking their child will "grow out" of this phase), some mistake bullying as assertiveness, while others see it as a growing problem that deserves an immediate response. Discovering that your child is being harassed, assaulted, tormented, or cyberbullied is one of the greatest nightmares for parents. They feel hopeless, fearful, angry, and deeply affected by the abuse their child is experiencing.

While it might seem simpler for some parents to just "ignore it" and think the bullying will pass, in most cases, it doesn't. Some students are hunted and bullied by their peers daily, and it can last for years, interrupting their studies, concentration, sleep patterns, self-esteem, and overall health. Therefore, it is very important for parents to detect the early warning signs of their child being a target of bullying or a bully.

The boxes below highlight some of these signs.

Signs that your child may be a bully:	Signs that your child may be a target:
• Seems eagerly excited about receiving a lot of attention and appears to thrive in it or gets angry when denied such attention • Often speaks egotistically, • drawing a larger-than-life image of himself/herself • Talks negatively about others, sometimes on personal matters like religion, race, family background, sexual orientation, etc.	• Withdrawal and mood changes • Loss of friends • Drop in grades • Loss of interest in participating in activities that were once fun • Change of attitude and behaviors, appearing extremely withdrawn or animated (hiding their sadness) • Physical signs: bruises, cuts • (self-mutilation), looking tired, etc.

Signs that your child may be a bully:	Signs that your child may be a target:
• Acts impulsively and feels the need to dominate others • Lacks empathy towards others and speaks as though they are superior to others (i.e., their peers).	• Health impact: they may get sick more often, fake an illness, develop eating disorders, have trouble sleeping at night, etc. • Signs of self-harm: they might start inflicting physical harm to themselves (e.g., cutting, scratching, biting, etc.)

PREVENTING BULLYING:
A Manual For Teachers In Promoting Global Educational Harmony

Parenting Tips: What to Do if Your Child is Being Bullied

The following steps should be DISCUSSED, PRACTICED & REPEATED for your child to effectively overcome bullying.

1. Be excited to see your child. Put your phone away, stop cooking or cleaning or working on work stuff, and give them a hug and a kiss when you greet them. This alone will comfort them.
2. Ask your child open-ended questions.
3. Listen without interruption and without giving advice right away. Silently listen to them. You must be calm, cool and collected because your anxiety will only amplify theirs. Make some tea and take time to listen, not try to FIX the situation.
4. Hold their hand, and just be with them. Show them physical affection.
5. Reassure them:
   - that this experience will only make them stronger.
   - that you promise you will always be there for them and that the bullying will eventually stop.
   - that bullying incidences usually last 37 seconds, so quickly move on to doing and being with people you love.
   - and remind them that bullying usually happens when there is an audience and when they are alone.
6. Brainstorm the HOT Spots and how to avoid those areas, where there is less adult supervision.
7. Discuss other people who have been bullied and *survived*. Here are some examples: Obama, Ellen DeGeneres, Oprah, me, you and millions of other teens and grownups who survived bullying!) – Watch: https://itgetsbetter.org/ (i.e., sharing inspirational stories).
8. Ask a friend or close relative to come over and speak with them. Someone they trust and look up to and love speaking to. (E.g., an older cousin. Say, "I need your help right now".) For single parents, reach out for help, even from one of your friends that can help inspire them.
9. Brainstorm and practice scenarios on how to respond to a bullying situation in the future. Role-play situations having them practice

using their assertive voice (e.g., repeat saying "STOP" at least 10 times). Let them yell and release built up emotions! Having anger is better than fear. Fear is crippling, but anger is empowering and has a higher vibration.
10. Role-play walking with confidence. Their posture is very important and can create an instant shift in their sense of self, calmness and confidence. Keeping their back straight, chin up, legs strong and shoulders rolled back will not only help their posture but also their mood. When shoulders are slouched, we automatically feel weaker. Standing up with our hands on the hips or up in the air in a V-pose (for 2 minutes) will increase testosterone levels in the body, making one feel like Superman or Wonder Woman. Try this and give positive feedback and reinforcement. Practice makes perfect.
11. Brainstorm with other friends at school whom they can connect or hang out with. The more friends they have, the more "protected" they may feel (i.e., like an army).
12. Discuss the 5 C's on how to make new friends:
    1. **Connect** – find things in common, make eye contact, smile and make jokes or small talk with someone you think is nice. Ask them, "Can I hang out with you?" or ask questions about schoolwork or their weekend. People love talking about themselves!
    2. **Compliment** – others' work, clothes, school project, or presentation.
    3. **Cooperate** – help someone out in class, show kindness (opening the door, lending your pencil), and get involved in a group or sports team.
    4. **Create** – something new; a skill, project, or campaign, and show it off
    5. **Care** for yourself (hygiene, power outfit = when you look good, you feel good, so go shopping with your child!).
13. Feed them healthy foods. Lots of fruits and vegetables or fish will uplift their inner spirits and make their bodies strong and alert (vs. pizza, pasta, and sugars).
14. Practice the **"STOP"** method:

PREVENTING BULLYING:
A Manual For Teachers In Promoting Global Educational Harmony

Before going to bed and before they start their day, they need to have a positive mind-set.

- **S**top. Close your eyes, sit with your back straight, and head up.
- **T**une in to your inner self and body. Take 3 deep breaths.
- **O**bserve your breath, heart rate and body temperature. Drink lots of water if needed.
- **P**erceive new possibilities and visualize the best outcome you would like to see happen.

Visualize and plan out the perfect day. See yourself walking with confidence. See yourself saying hello and laughing with your friends. Children cannot expect a new outcome with the same old patterns. They need to develop a new, more balanced self with a new set of habits. Write affirmations or positive quotes in your room and in your mirror. (Example: Life is just getting better, thank you, thank you, thank you!)

On the weekend:

- Connect with other parents (reach out) or invite some friends and family members over. Feed them. Eat and laugh together. Share stories of their bullying experiences—everyone has some.
- Bring your child to a cultural event in your community or go volunteering at a homeless center, cancer wellness center or any place that will help them see other people's struggles and how they can be of assistance. Having a feeling of significance and value in society will immediately increase their self-worth.

Also, it is very important for children to remember their positive qualities, so it can be helpful to have them write in a journal or discuss the following:

    a. What are 5–10 positive traits, skills and characteristics that they have?

    b. How will they stand up for themselves if the bullying happens again?

    c. What was good about their day (focusing on the positive and feelings of gratitude)?

    d. What were the WOW Moments (coolest moments) of their day?
    e. What are they most grateful for even though the bullying incident occurred? What is the greatest learning they have from this experience?

At home:

- Play positive, uplifting or relaxing music in the background at home to ease their stress level.
- Avoid violent television programs. Monitor cell phone and Internet use, and who they trust online among their so-called friends.
- Play a board game. Don't leave them alone with their thoughts.
- Go for a walk in nature and get fresh air for at least 45 minutes and at least 1-3 times a week.
- Ask them to help you do something fun like cooking or washing your car, organize their room and put those affirmations on the wall, or go to a senior's home and ask them about bullying.

What parents can do on their own time: ***

- Call and email teachers, counselors, and principals. Allow this to be *confidential* so your child does not panic more. Give them solutions such as:
    - pairing your child for a project or class activity with one of the positive leaders in class, and to follow up with you after it is done.
    - emailing the gym teacher to pair your child with a strong leader to support them or to get involved in a sport that would build their confidence and circle of friends.
    - emailing the bus driver or school recess monitor to keep an eye on your child and sit close to them and keep a check-in for a few days.
    - asking if a child from an older grade can help support or hang out with your child.

- getting the phone number of any parent in the same grade who is willing to help you out and play together on the weekend or go see a movie or have pizza.
- starting or looking for a Parent Support Group or Committee (with Q & A's) on Facebook or the school's website or platform. Bullying prevention is a community-wide effort. Don't be afraid to ask for help. Parents all share your concern and love to help!!!!

Email the bully's parents directly, *kindly* asking them to discuss their child's behavior and relationship with your child.

- Avoid threats because these can be used against you.
- Sometimes parents have no idea that their child is a bully, so informing them may be helpful. Parents who are notified that their child is behaving in an uncivilized manner must also keep their cool and avoid any physical punishments, which will only generate more anger in the child, and use logical consequences to reinforce positive behaviors.
- Watch your own behaviors and speech. Remember that bullying is a learned behavior. The way you speak to your work colleagues, spouse or family reflects in how your children will speak to others at school.

If the school doesn't help and the bullying continues after months or years of difficulty, here are some alternatives:

- Consider changing schools or moving.
- Make an appointment with a psychologist; it is worth the cost.
- Develop resilience by learning taekwondo, karate, self-defense, kickboxing, exercise, yoga, etc.

Lastly, for parents who have experienced bullying or who have lost their child due to cyberbullying or any other forms, I encourage you to use your voice and continue paying it forward by helping other parents who have a child affected by bullying.

How to Respond to Cyberbullying

1. Take a deep breath, exhale slowly 3 times, and drink some water.
2. Save the photo, text, video, email, or documentation.
3. Show and report to the school administration or guidance counselor, parents and/or the police (911).
4. Block the abuser ASAP. *Don't let your mind or precious eyes see any more of that nonsense!*
5. Do not respond or add fuel to the fire. That is what they want.
6. Talk about it to members of your family, like your aunts and uncles, cousins or grandparents.
7. Do not post your problems on Facebook, Messenger, Twitter or Instagram because it shows your vulnerability and makes you more of a target.
8. Eat healthy (fruits that will uplift you vs. pizza, chips and burgers).
9. Exercise. Meditate.
10. Watch funny movies.
11. Go for a brisk walk in nature, then do yoga.
12. Play your favorite uplifting songs.
13. Seek affection from friends and family.
14. Let it go by changing your mind—fast!
15. Understand the psychology of a bully's harmful behavior:
    a. Family structure (parental neglect, single parenting, divorce, drugs, alcohol)
    b. Socio-economic or financial issues
    c. Mental health issues (depression, anxiety, bipolar disorder or PTSD)
    d. Exposure to violence in real life or in the media
    e. Neglect by teachers or peers; wanting attention
    f. They were bullied (targets)

*"When another person makes you suffer, it is because **he suffers deeply within himself**, and his suffering is spilling over. He does not need punishment; he needs help. That's the message he is sending."* — Thich Nhat Han

SECTION 3

PREVENTION & RESPONSE STRATEGIES FOR EDUCATORS

PREVENTING BULLYING:
A Manual For Teachers In Promoting Global Educational Harmony

To ignore bullying is to tolerate it.

How much do you know your students and what's really going on in their lives? What percentage of your time do you spend really listening to your students? How much 1-1 time are you giving each student? How are your relationships with each of them? Which students do you speak to least and why do you think that is? How might you try to build bonds and check-in with those students? Not only will you be sending a positive message in the class by speaking to the student whom you don't give much attention to, but you will also send a positive message, allowing everyone to feel appreciated.

Do you remember high school? Were you one of the lucky ones not affected by bullying, or were you the one on the opposite side, being bullied at times? Do you remember watching others being bullied around you? It's never too late. You too can heal your past by getting involved now.

Don't forget why you became a teacher, which was probably to make a difference, share your passion, and positively impact the lives of the future generations. It all begins in your classroom with simple activities, group discussions, a little love, time management, openness, and risk-taking on everyone's part. Only then will we be closer to our goal and help put an end to bullying.

Questions to Consider Before Your Bullying Prevention Initiatives

1. Does your school support your initiatives on implementing this prevention program? If not, it is recommended to notify directors of the activities and intervention strategies you will be applying.
2. Do your students know their school's code of conduct against bullying behaviors and the sanction involved? If not, please share them with constant reminders in the promotion of kindness, friendships, and respect for one another.
3. What type of bullying mainly occurs at your school and with your students? Use the "Bullying Assessment Questionnaire" to gain some knowledge of what issues are occurring most.
4. Have you witnessed or heard about any bullying occurrences? If so, what did you do? How did you feel?
5. Have you ever reported a bullying incident to school administrators? What was their reaction and how effective was their intervention? Was there any positive progress on behalf of the student? Did anyone follow up with the bully or target or have a group intervention with those involved so the target feels safe to come to school during this emotional time?
6. What is your current emotional readiness for dealing with students' bullying problems? It's important that you are well-balanced and capable to teach this topic only if you feel you are able.
7. When might you integrate these activities into your schedule and course development? Open your calendar and try to plan some dates where you can integrate some of these activities and group discussions.
8. How strong are the student relationships in your class? Is everyone friendly and amicable? Do they really know and respect one another for who they are? This is very important. Ask students to go into groups of 3–4 (with their friends or people they know) and watch the way they form their own cliques and who is left out. You will often see the loners and ones in smaller groups; you will automatically know they might be a target of bullying.

9. What are some things you can do to make everyone feel safe, comfortable, and more respected this week in your class?
10. How are your student-teacher relationships? Are you approachable and available? Can a student confide in you? Do students have your office hours or email if they ever need to contact you for help?

Identifying Students' Needs

"Educators cannot change or teach someone if they judge or label them. They need to care and understand their world."

Addressing students' basic needs is monumental when trying to teach and prevent bullying. The *Glory of Education's* Bullying Prevention Program is based on an understanding of our six basic needs and its application on how to educate on and prevent bullying in the classroom.

Students' Six basic needs:

BOUNDARIES	LOVE	SAFETY
SIGNIFICANCE	VARIETY	GROWTH & CONTRIBUTION

1. Providing students with rules, regulations, and **BOUNDARIES** to promote the benefits of learning and respecting each other. In other words, students need clear guidelines as to where the line stops and what limits they can and cannot cross. Therefore, it is essential to define the school guidelines, rules, and sanctions when it involves bullying.
2. Giving them **LOVE** by building relationships and friendships through group activities and discussions, where they create bonds and feel a stronger connection between each other without judgment.
3. Providing them with absolute certainty that they are in a **SAFE** learning environment and if bullying occurs, sanctions will be made and enforced.
4. Making them feel **SIGNIFICANT** in that their words are heard, and their presence matter among others. Our goal is that the activities provided in this manual, in due time, will give them an opportunity to develop their own self-confidence.
5. Offering them **VARIETY** in the way their classes are taught, including didactic learning activities, role plays, open discussions,

true or false games and small group work, addressing students' needs and various learning styles.
6. Creating an environment of **PERSONAL GROWTH** and **CONTRIBUTION**, where students are involved in the learning process and feel good about it.

Student Learning Outcomes:

1. I feel safe.
2. I understand the rules.
3. I understand bullying.
4. I feel empathy for others.
5. I have better peer relations.
6. I gained conflict resolution skills.
7. I am a leader and an advocate against bullying.

How to Recognize Your Students' Roles in Bullying

From an educator's perspective, you can often tell if your student is a **target of bullying** by observing their behavior and attitude. Here are some signs that your student may be a target:

- Difficulty concentrating in class/daydreaming
- Absenteeism/skipping classes
- Lack of participation/difficulty speaking when addressed
- Being an outsider (loner)/may sit by self during lunch or not be included in group or class activities
- Appearing depressed or afraid
- Showing signs of physical abuse or self-harm

Signs that your student may be a **bully**:

- Overly confident
- Rude and/or aggressive/arrogant
- Popular or leader of the class/always surrounded by friends
- Angry or frustrated /larger-than-life; may belittle you (as the educator) or fellow classmates "jokingly"

Signs that your student may be a **bystander**:

- Seems neutral and uninvolved/goes along with the crowd
- Takes a protective stance/tries to protect self over others
- Is a quiet onlooker/doesn't say much
- Is an encourager or friend of the bully/doesn't stop cruel jokes from being made

"Dealing with challenging people helps to build character." — Joel Osteen

PREVENTING BULLYING:
A Manual For Teachers In Promoting Global Educational Harmony

The Glory of Education's 7 Step Bullying Prevention Model

"If we all did a little, this world would be a better place." — Christina Theophilos

The classroom-based learning activities provided in this manual have been designed to follow a sequential seven-step learning model. This model assists teachers on how to effectively execute their lessons with comfort and ease, and in turn, properly educate students in making better decisions on how to respond to bullying. If each teacher integrates some time (preferably 1 hour each month) into their course curriculum, you will see a change in your entire school climate and create one of the most positive learning environments for students to excel in and realize their dreams.

Step 1: Set a Harmonious Tone in the Classroom
Create a non-threatening classroom environment where students feel calm, safe, and at ease; make sure that the lines of communication are opened and that trust and positive affirmations about each other are cultivated and explored among peers. Setting the tone creates a harmonious balance where students want to be there and participate. Identifying students' personal needs and values should also be addressed at this stage.

Activity #1: Promote Respect for Self and Others Using the "I Am Mantra"

Activity #2: Encouraging Incantations

Activity #3: Identifying Our Basic Human Needs

Activity # 4: Practice the Art of Listening

Activity #5: Establish Trust Discussion and Exercises

Activity #6: Understanding E.M.P.A.T.H.Y

Step 2: Create Respectful Ground Rules

Provide students with structured ground rules that enable them to communicate their ideas and opinions in a thoughtful, respectful, and succinct manner. This part of the program discusses school conduct guidelines and sanctions. In order to achieve classroom management during a session, it is suggested to review the "Great Listening Skills" activity as a guide on how to ensure students' attentiveness.

Activity #7: Feel the Positivity and Sing

Activity #8: Brainstorm Respectful Do's and Don'ts

Activity #9: Appropriate Code of Conduct and Sanctions Forms

Activity #10: Applying the Great Listening Skills and Classroom Management

Step 3: Raise Students' Awareness about Bullying

Helping clarify students' awareness about bullying and identifying its various forms is essential at this stage. Our objective here is for students to identify with their role in bullying as a target, bystander, or bully. Educators must shift the way students view themselves and the way they think about others, by integrating thought-provoking questions, open discussions, and didactic activities provided below:

Activity #11: Identifying What's Cool and Uncool?

Activity #12: Defining Bullying

Activity #13: Opening Class Discussion about Bullying

Activity #14: Bullying Word Association (Icebreaker)

Activity #15: True or False — Identifying Students' Opinions about Bullying

Step 4: Cultivate Moments of Empathy and Morality

In order to change students' behaviors and the way they feel about bullying, it is essential to utilize an experiential learning approach, encompassing exercises and activities where students can experience true empathy and feel empowered to help stop bullying. It is most important at this stage for students (and bullies in particular) to learn first-hand how it feels to be on the receiving end of bullying (done sensitively and systematically), so they are motivated to treat others as they would want to be treated themselves.

Activity #16: "Step Up If" — Identifying Student Commonalities

Activity #17: Write Your Truth about Bullying and Post It Anonymously

Activity #18: Walk in Their Shoes: An Experiential Learning Exercise

Activity #19: Exploring Bullying Roles and Small Group Discussion

Activity #20: The Use and Abuse of Power Round Circle Discussion

Activity #21: Understanding the Effects of Bullying

Step 5: Eliminate the Motivation to Bully by Building Peer Relations

Helping students get to know each other better and finding things in common can reduce the motivation to bully. This process can be achieved by putting students into groups with peers they hardly know or have not spoken to in great depth. The following activities enable students to be heard, healed, and accepted for who they really are, in hopes that they will create bonds with their peers and find that they are more alike than unlike and are struggling with similar insecurities and human needs, which ultimately leads to feeling safe, loved and accepted.

Activity #22: "I feel... when..." Sharing Feelings Activity

Activity #23: Identifying Students' Actions and Values

Activity #24: Student Confessions: Are You a Bully, Bystander, Helper, or Target?

Activity #25: The Masks We Wear!

Activity #26: Sharing Personal Stories of Pain and Healing

Activity #27: "If You Really Knew Me"

Activity #28: Admitting Our Mistakes

Step 6: Provide Opportunities to Practice Conflict Resolution and Interpersonal Skills

We all know that practice makes perfect. Therefore, students must learn how to handle bullying situations by practicing conflict resolution strategies. They need to be trained as if it was their second nature to help one another and defend themselves. Practicing assertiveness using role-plays, debates, and other interpersonal skills can greatly influence students' confidence for when and if a bullying situation arises. Targets and bystanders need to feel empowered to stand up for themselves or those around them, just as much as bullies need to understand that their abusive behaviors are not acceptable, nor will be tolerated by others.

Activity #29: Apologizing to Those You Hurt

Activity #30: Forgiveness vs. Holding Grudges

Activity #31: Identifying Where Bullies Bully and How to Respond

Activity #32: Role-Playing Activity

Activity #33: Understanding Disrespectful Behaviors: How Would You feel?

Activity 34: Bullying Scenarios: What Would You Do? (Dealing with Confrontation)

Step 7: Encourage Leadership by Getting Students Involved in the Prevention Process

When students participate in the bullying prevention process—whether it is from performing a skit, class presentation, creating a poster or poem, or partaking in a mentorship program—advocacy against bullying will naturally arise. Everyone enjoys doing acts of kindness for others, but oftentimes, students need guidance on how to do so. Students must be given the opportunity to think about what they could do for the betterment of their society and/or school community. Providing students with an incentive to do good will not only enhance their self-esteem, but it will also enable students to learn about teamwork and leadership in their efforts towards a common and positive goal.

Activity #35: Debating Bullying Topics

Activity #36: Give and Receive Compliments

Activity #37: Launch the Creation of Their Goals

Activity #38: Defining True Leadership

Activity #39: Define Authentic Leadership

Activity #40: Get Students Involved in the Prevention Process

Activity #41: Anti-Bullying Design Flyers

Activity #42: Make an Anti-Bullying Pledge and Certificate of Understanding

Activity Layout and Design

This manual is designed to ensure that educators are clear on the goal, time, materials, procedures, processing questions, and key take-away message for each activity provided. Below is an explanation of each activity's layout design:

Activity Title:

Activity goal: Activities start off elaborating on the goal of the exercise, how it fits in with the broader bullying prevention program, and how the exercise will be beneficial to students.

Approximate activity time: Sets an approximate time for the completion of the activity. This can vary depending on how long one can engage students in the exercise and during the post- activity discussion session. Remember, the activity length will depend on the educator's discretion. For example, if an exercise appears to be engaging students and encouraging participation, it might be good to allow students extra time to complete their thoughts and to express their opinions. Other activities in which students don't appear to be as comfortable or engaged can be limited, with the educator taking a greater role in expanding on the activity goal or choosing another depending on the group's atmosphere.

Materials required: All activities list out materials required for the exercise at the beginning to aid educators in planning out the activity. Most activities do not require any materials apart from photocopies that can easily be written by hand if a photocopy machine isn't available. These materials provide a convenient visual aid for the exercise.

Step-by-step activity process: A step-by-step guide is provided for each activity on how to execute the exercise, along with any required charts/graphs/diagrams (mentioned in the 'materials required' section). This guide quickly familiarizes busy teachers with what the activity encompasses and clearly lays out the expectations from the students and facilitators. It is a good idea for all facilitators/teachers to do a quick read of the step-by-step section to ensure they are aware of what needs to be done prior to executing the activity.

Post-activity discussion questions: Upon completion of an activity, it is strongly recommended for educators to allow time to discuss any last feelings, questions, or concerns students may have. Make time and use post-activity processing questions, even if that means cutting the activity short. Despite the large group dynamic being intimidating and students possibly feeling "exposed," it is a good opportunity for extroverted students to express themselves or the stories and feelings of their small group members, thus making everyone feel involved. Finally, having a large group discussion enables diverse perspectives to be brought together as a whole, where students can express themselves, learn and inspire one another.

Examples of Post-activity processing questions:

1. What do you think the purpose of this activity was?
2. What did you enjoy the most from this session? And what did you not like?
3. What else did you learn from this activity?
4. What was most difficult for you during this session?
5. Can you suggest ways of improving this activity?

Key take-away message: The activity is wrapped up by a key takeaway message. This message is aimed at providing "food for thought" and closing remarks to be read by the teacher and possibly shared with the entire class.

Christina Theophilos, M.Ed. & Raju Ramanathan, M.Tech

Benefits of Classroom-Based Learning Activities

"I hear and I forget. I see and I remember. I do and I understand." — Chinese Proverb

For students, the following activities in this manual will:

- Address their need to discuss topics that they are interested in and might be experiencing.
- Provide and assist students' understanding of bullying and its forms, causes and solutions.
- Increase students' awareness of self and others.
- Enable students to discuss, learn and listen to their peers (i.e., those whose opinions they care about) in a comfortable and safe environment.
- Instill consciousness that they are not alone in their struggles.
- Help form a social support group and a safe place to share their problems.
- Encourage teamwork and facilitate improved group dynamics.
- Build closer relationships and friendships among peers.
- Provide fun activities for all students' needs and various learning styles.
- Build skills in self-defense, assertiveness and helping others.
- Provide processing questions after each activity to ensure clarity, reflection, and emotional growth.
- Provide an opportunity to get involved in the solution and alternatives to the violence.
- Promote self-confidence, respect and kindness.
- Prevent teen depression, suicidal thoughts and actions.
- Prevent heartaches, stress and continuation of violent abuse.

In short, the activities aim to help students overcome and prevent:

- Bullying, discrimination.
- Violence.

PREVENTING BULLYING:
A Manual For Teachers In Promoting Global Educational Harmony

- Social rejection, gossiping.
- Low self-esteem.
- Poor academic achievements.
- Depression.
- Thoughts of suicide or revenge.
- Segregation.
- Ethnocentrism.
- Prejudice, homophobia.
- Absenteeism.
- Cutting/self-mutilation.

For *schools*, this manual will:

- Address school needs and concerns regarding their students' well-being.
- Reduce the likelihood of bullying in and outside of schools.
- Encourage a safe school environment.
- Provide abundant resources suited to class needs.
- Encourage a positive group atmosphere and learning environment.
- Increase students' ability to focus on academic subjects and overall grades.

Schools will save costs on:

- Hiring external speakers, specialists, programs, and interventions.
- Government health services.

For educators, this manual provides:

- A bullying overview, including:
  - ✓ Contributing factors.
  - ✓ Cyberbullying.
  - ✓ Who is at risk.
  - ✓ Current problems in combating this bullying phenomenon.

- School Involvement Strategies, including:
  - ✓ Seven steps for developing your school's action plan.
  - ✓ Assessment forms.
  - ✓ Information.
  - ✓ Letters to parents.

- Teacher's Aid for Bullying Prevention, including:
  - ✓ A seven-step prevention program.
  - ✓ Facilitation and intervention strategies.
  - ✓ Quick tips for each core subject.

- Prevention and Response Program and Student Learning Activities involving:

  - ✓ Group discussions, exercises, games, and projects that evoke incredible learning experiences to help students' emotional well-being.

The Importance of Making Random Groups

Bullies usually hang out with students who reinforce their negative behavior. Therefore, it is important to separate the students who act aggressively and mix them up with those whom they do not know too well or who aren't bullies. By mixing up groups, you will allow the target to be placed in an environment that will include those who might stand up for them, rather than into another bullying situation.

It is important to monitor students' reactions to the formation of group processes because the last thing that you want is a bully working with his or her target, which might make matters worse for the target if problems are unresolved or ongoing. Therefore, it is recommended to have the groups prepare before the class, and even the chair and table arrangements. If the groups are separated once the class has begun, and the cliques have already formed, it will be most difficult to separate them and remove their security blankets.

Therefore, having students stand outside the class door and assigning new seating positions for a few classes *that you have created* (i.e., with their names written on a piece of paper on their assigned desks) will reinforce your authority and force them into collaborating with peers and hopefully make new friends. Mixing up the introverts, jocks, and rebellious kids is good for everyone to get to know each other and find commonalities.

The activities provided in this manual are intended to help students grow and learn from their peers, especially those they less frequently interact with. Forming random groups is essential and will help to ensure equal distribution and the highest likelihood of diversity in peer-group assignments, generating a variance in their interactions. Students will be challenged and have a greater sense of connectedness than if they were simply partnered up with friends or common "cliques," and no one will feel left out as the "last one chosen." Studies show that when people are placed with those they don't know well (i.e., those who are outside of their immediate social circle), they are more likely to share stories, step out of their comfort zone, and get actively engaged.

How to Make Random Groups

1. **Draw names**: Write the names of each student on a piece of paper and put them all in a bag or small box. Next, draw the names and read them out loud, dividing them into the number of groups needed.
2. **Group Popsicle sticks**: At your local craft store, buy wooden popsicle sticks and write your students names on each stick. Then, randomly call out names that will form a group.
3. **Birthday or zodiac sign grouping**: Have students stand in a line according to either their birth month (January to December) or height (from tallest to shortest). Next, the teacher selects the number of students needed per group from those standing next to each other in this line.
4. **First names**: Have students stand in line in alphabetical order according to their first names (A: Alfred to Z: Zoe). Next, the teacher selects the number of students needed per group from those standing next to each other in this line.
5. **Assign a number**: Make students stand in a line and call out a number in sequential order according to the number of groups needed (i.e., 1 followed by 2 then 3 and so on). Ask students to remember their number and move to the side of the room where their number applies.
6. **Give a letter or number** to each student (e.g., A-B-C or 1-2-3 for groups of three) Have students choose a number or letter from the "random group assignment box or bag" created by the teacher to determine which group they belong to.
7. **Blindly choose a color and group**: Assign groups to 4 different colors by randomly distributing or having each student blindly choose one of the four colors. (e.g., Red, Yellow, Blue and Green).
8. **Siblings or only child**: Have students divide into 3 groups according to: (1) single/only child, (2) one sibling, (3) two or more siblings. Redistribute to make even, if needed.

Essential Facilitation Tips Before Teaching Anti-Bullying

Prepare yourself by considering the following bullying prevention guidelines:

1. <u>Get administrative support</u>. Set specific goals and create an action plan.
2. <u>Notify parents</u> that you are getting involved and using this program to avoid any legalities, using the "Bullying Prevention & Awareness Letter to Parents" provided in SECTION 2.
3. <u>Encourage other teachers and staff to be involved</u>. Divide learning activities with other teachers, so that the entire school can collaboratively make positive initiatives.
4. <u>Integrate, plan, and set aside some time in your class curriculum</u> for the learning activities and notify students about when you will discuss this important subject, so that they too are emotionally and mentally prepared.
5. <u>Review SECTION 1: Bullying Overview</u>, which will better prepare you for the subject (i.e., root causes, influences, outcomes, solution, etc.).
6. <u>Do your research</u> before discussing bullying prevention with your class. Find out if there are any issues from the school counselor (e.g., name-calling, malicious gossip, incidents related to bullying, etc.).
7. <u>Assess students' specific needs</u> by distributing the "Bullying Assessment Questionnaire" provided.
8. <u>Get to know your students</u> in order to adapt your session based on your students' needs and/or experiences. Talk with your students prior to or after class and build connections with them. This will allow them to feel more comfortable and approach you if they need to confide in you about a bullying situation.
9. <u>Hang uplifting and positive posters</u>, stories, or quotes of inspirational and admirable role models that will help set a positive tone in the classroom.
10. <u>Set up the room</u>. Changing the standard classroom layout for this session will make students think of it as something different and not part of their regular class sessions. Rearrange chairs, desks,

and/or tables for small group work and large group discussion. Try to form a closed circle at times to build a sense of solidarity, unity, and open sharing space.

11. <u>Play soothing music in the background to help set the tone</u> of the class and give students some privacy between other groups. (E.g., if they are working in groups, put some upbeat music; if they are working alone brainstorming or sharing stories in pairs, add some reflective tunes.)
12. <u>Don't be afraid of the bullies</u>. Here is a chance for you to redesign and reprogram their minds into ones that are more loving and more compassionate towards themselves and others. The key is to see each of them in their "highest light" and full potential of being the kind, caring, and compassionate beings that we truly are.
13. <u>Remember that the goal is to INCREASE students' SELF-ESTEEM</u>, which is the root cause of bullying. Those who are bullies are often hurting deeply inside, subconsciously allowing their pain to overflow onto others, and using the target(s) as their punching bag, which is not right.
14. <u>Have students engage in deep breathing exercises before each session</u> for them to tap into their higher, most genuine, and authentic selves, which is divine love. Allow them to look inside at what is really hurting them, and then to let go, breathe, and forgive themselves and others who have hurt them. Simply guiding them to sit up straight, close their eyes, and take three deep breaths while exhaling slowly, will settle their mind and turbulent emotions. See SECTION 5 and Activity 1 on Mindful Meditation techniques.
15. <u>Print, read, and discuss the "School Code of Conduct" and "School Sanctions"</u> (provided), which will help clarify acceptable and unacceptable student behaviors.
16. <u>Set ground rules and be prepared.</u> Feel free to adapt material according to your teaching style and students' needs. Give clear instructions with the aid of an overhead projector or distribute detailed handouts of the activity. Incorporate the **"The Effective Listening Techniques"** before each lesson to get their full attention and respect.

17. <u>Ask students</u> to clarify the goal of the exercise to ensure group understanding. Distribute and discuss your school's code of conduct and sanctions.
18. **Choose an activity that YOU FEEL comfortable with**. Put yourself in their shoes and think about what activity would also be best for your students—one that you feel mentally and emotionally prepared to teach and ensures the greatest impact. Also, remember to design your session plan appropriately by carefully selecting activities considering these factors:
    - Gender: Do you have more young males or females in your class?
    - Age and Maturity: Do your students have the emotional capacity and comprehension ability to participate in the exercise?
    - Demographic: Is your school in a rural or urban community?

Starting Your Session:

A. <u>Establish authority.</u> You must always maintain control of the group and the discussions. You should direct who participates, ensuring that what students are sharing is relevant to the context, while monitoring the duration of the session. Do not accept any insults towards other students while they share their stories. As a facilitator, showing any subtle approval for anti-social statements such as name-calling or abusive language towards a person or group will reinforce negative behavior. In other words, tolerating sexist, homophobic, or racist language is counterproductive to the group's learning.)

B. <u>Promote the right attitude.</u> Be passionate, serious, non-judgmental, and educated, and try to have fun. Look at your students when they speak to you and show interest in what they are expressing. Remember that body language communicates almost ninety percent of what we say. Crossing your arms, turning red, or raising an eyebrow can all show signs of your comfort level and attitude.

C. <u>Promote respect.</u> If a student is laughed at or made fun of, it is essential that the facilitator address the situation immediately. Do not tolerate rude or negative behavior as this will only aggravate the situation and make students feel threatened and hesitant to participate or ask questions.

D. <u>Minimize WHY questions as these put students on the defensive.</u> Ask HOW or WHAT instead. (Example: "Why do people feel this way?" VS. "What motivates people to feel this way?")

E. <u>Encourage participation.</u> In order to increase group participation, thank those who share their stories and opinions. This will make students feel that their thoughts are valued and appreciated, encouraging others to provide their feedback as well. Please, remember to respect those who do not wish to participate either due to cultural, religious, social, or personal reasons. Also, students may want to take some time to gather their thoughts before they respond. Let them do this by allowing them some "quiet time" to gather their thoughts and opinions.

F. <u>Respond to bullying situations</u> using certain bullying "response" activities suggested. **Don't let "teachable moments" pass you by.** Do not be afraid to address uncomfortable situations or remarks. These are golden opportunities that will have great impact on all students involved or witnessing bullying. Breathe, take your time, and share your knowledge. React to a bullying situation by using the "Intervention Strategies & Guidelines."

Finishing Up:

G. <u>Have an "anonymous question box"</u> for students to drop their questions in, either before or after class. This can encourage students to express their concerns, issues, and feelings more openly, knowing that they cannot be directly identified by their peers.

H. <u>Say "My door is always open" and give referrals</u> to a counselor or specialist if necessary. Contact your school's guidance counselor for some emergency numbers or hotlines.

SECTION 4

INTERVENTION STRATEGIES

Classroom Management Techniques

> *"Good teachers inform, while great teachers transform lives."* — Raju Ramanathan

Teaching *adolescents* any subject can be challenging. When teaching youth such an important and delicate subject such as bullying prevention, it is important to set a positive, calm, and trusting tone in the class for teaching and learning to flourish. The following classroom management tips will help create this tone and clarify some significant rules of behavior. Without these standards and expectations in place, there is room for student chaos, uncertainty, fear, and disorder. Research shows that students who received disciplinary interventions and effective classroom management techniques had a more powerful impact on students' achievement scores.

Therefore, in order to enhance student learning, teachers are suggested to:

1. **Connect with your students** by getting to know them, asking them about their weekend before or after class (small talk), increasing your proximity, saying their name, making eye contact (i.e., for over 2 seconds), and complimenting their efforts.
2. Make wise choices about the **most effective instructional strategies** and group activities that can be used (i.e., cooperative vs. individual learning) that will best support their learning.
3. Design a classroom curriculum to **facilitate student learning** (i.e., articulating proper sequence, presentation, and pacing of their content, considering students' collective and individual needs).

4. Use effective classroom management techniques that:
   a. include **classroom rules** that involve group input.
   b. have students understand, **appreciate and commit** to the **rules**.[1]
   c. encourage and reinforce appropriate behavior.

*"When you approach **responsibility** and **learning** with a **positive attitude**, your ability to listen and tune-in will automatically increase as well."* — Raju Ramanathan

---

[1] Marzano, R. J., Marzano, J. S., and Pickering, D. (2003). Classroom management that works: Research-based strategies for every teacher. Alexandria, VA: Association for Supervision and Curriculum Development.

PREVENTING BULLYING:
A Manual For Teachers In Promoting Global Educational Harmony

Suggestions on Setting Ground Rules

"Students need to internalize their teacher's expectation of them, so they can be independent learners."

1. Lay down the **ground rules early on** (i.e., Day 1). This is a *critical* first step.
2. The rules should be **clear, positively stated**, and ones that you are willing to enforce. Students will be observing your authority and make judgments about how they can behave.

   3–6 rules are recommended:

   - **Example A:** (1) Respect others, (2) Be on time, (3) Be prepared, and (4) Do not interrupt when others are speaking.
   - **Example B:** (1) Say hello and smile when you walk into class, (2) Show kindness to others, and (3) Choose your words with care and compassion.
   - **Example C: Teach the 3 A's vs. the 3 Cs.**
     - Appreciate, Acknowledge, and Attention/Affection (i.e., that will automatically and naturally create positive emotions) versus:
     - Criticizing, Condemning, and Complaining (i.e., that will automatically generate negative emotions)
3. Discuss the importance of each rule and what they mean specifically (e.g., what does "respecting your peers" look like?), making sure they understand them.
4. Post the rules in a large font at the front of the classroom. Leave the rules in the class where students can see them.
5. If a student still breaks the rule, remind them of the rules, point to it, or even ask them to read the rules (out loud).
6. Optional: Have students read and sign a contract, which includes class rules and regulations.
7. Let students know the sanctions of their behavior (e.g., grade/participation)

8. Do not use corporal or group punishments.
9. Do not use harsh or extremely embarrassing punishments. Our goal is to increase a student's self-esteem, not crush it.
10. Have students choose a "logical consequence" for their misbehavior.
11. Help them understand the negative impact of their behaviors on class learning.
12. Suggest a more appropriate way of behaving under the circumstances.
13. Decide when to take action, i.e., "3 strikes and you're out." Examples of some consequences include being sent to the principal's office; being unable to attend fun class activities; being seated in a secluded area of the room where they cannot distract you or others, such as sitting facing the wall; detention; verbal apology; points taken off; and phone call to parents.

Using the 3 R's: Recognize, React and Resolve a Bullying Situation

Utilize the Three Guiding Principles:

These *three guiding principles* encompass a simple approach to handling bullying for educators. The first step is *recognizing* that a bullying incident has occurred. The second step is *reacting* to the occurrence in a positive manner and the third step is to *resolve* the situation.

The three guiding principles:

1. RECOGNIZE: Signs, types, and symptoms of bullying
   - Observe the situation and recognize it promptly.
   - Be on the lookout for early signs such as teasing, name-calling, or exclusion, which may avoid later problems of verbal, nonverbal, or physical aggression.
   - Trust your instincts and use your judgment.
   - Assess and approach the situation with care and caution.

2. REACT: Immediately and Professionally
   - React immediately. Stop it in its tracks. Don't wait until it's a full-blown situation.
   - Let the bully, bystanders, and targets know that this behavior is not acceptable and will not be tolerated in or outside the classroom.
   - Intervene using a "Non-aggressive, No Blame Approach."
   - Talk to the students who were involved in a 1-1 basis. Be wary of group dynamics that are likely to favor the bully.
   - Give the "Bullying Reflection Sheet" to the bully and review responses together.
   - Submit the "Heads Up Form" to school authorities notifying them of the situation and discussions held.

3. <u>RESOLVE: With Compassion and Understanding</u>
    - Follow up and evaluate the bullying incident in a timely fashion.
    - Provide words of encouragement to the bully. Give them feedback on how you appreciate their effort in modifying their undesirable behavior (i.e., positive reinforcement).
    - Bullies often have underlying issues that are complex and may require long-term support and positive reinforcement for permanent change.
    - Strategies for eliminating the bullying behavior must be individualized, long-term, and broad-based because changing a behavior permanently takes time.
    - The consequences of bullying must be well-established and understood and applied in an immediate and consistent manner. Encouraging formative responsibility development, in line with the consistent application of realistic consequences over the long term, will enhance positive behavior, skill development, and a greater understanding of empathy.

PREVENTING BULLYING:
A Manual For Teachers In Promoting Global Educational Harmony

How to Resolve a Bullying Situation in Class

If a bullying incident takes place during class, teachers must feel prepared to act immediately. Below are some guidelines you can refer to when addressing bullying. Remember to customize your approach depending on the specific situation and your familiarity with the students' background to help put the situation in context.

1. Inform the bully and class that their behavior or abuse is unacceptable and will not be tolerated.
2. Ask the bully to see you after class to discuss further and/or expel the student from your class using the *"Heads Up Form"* (provided below) notifying parents and school authorities. Reinforce the Zero Tolerance for Bullying school policy.
3. Tell students to monitor their peers' behaviors and report all forms of bullying. Remind them that they are allowing bullying to continue by being bystanders and doing nothing.
4. Vocalize to the entire class that bullying and all forms of abuse (i.e., verbal, non-verbal, physical, cyber, and sexual abuse) are wrong, against school policy, and *illegal*.
5. Offer students your email address and the counselor's location to report an abuse.
6. Distribute the *"Student Misconduct Reflection Sheet"* (provided below) and ask the student to complete the sheet outside the class and return it with their parents' signature.
7. Take a break to recompose yourself and ask students to read or study for a few minutes to reflect on the incident. Next, either continue your lesson or discuss the situation with the entire class using one of the activities provided. Follow up and review pro- social behavior in the next class and review class rules and sanctions.

Reporting Misconduct to Authorities: "Heads Up" Form

Student Referral to Administration

Student Name:	Date:
Referred by:	Class/Program:

Sanctions and plans to improve student behavior include:

Teacher's Name: _____

Signature: _____

PREVENTING BULLYING:
A Manual For Teachers In Promoting Global Educational Harmony

Student Misconduct Reflection Sheet

Name: _____ Date: _____

    a.   Summarize the incident you were involved in.
_____
_____

    b.   What motivated you to say or do the things you did?
_____
_____

    c.   How do you think you made other people that were involved in this situation feel?
_____
_____

    d.   How would you feel and react if the tables were turned and someone did the same thing to you?
_____
_____

    e.   What would have been a better alternative for getting your feelings or point across?
_____
_____

    f.   What will you do next to rectify the situation?
_____
_____

    g.   What are some logical consequences and sanctions for your actions?
_____
_____

Parent/Guardian Signature: _____

Date: _____

CHRISTINA THEOPHILOS, M.ED. & RAJU RAMANATHAN, M.TECH

How to Have Meaningful Student Interventions

"71% of teachers say they usually intervene with bullying problems; but only 25% of students say that teachers intervene." [2]

As educators, we must be proactive and not be afraid of getting involved in a bullying situation that might help all those involved, including the bully, who is also suffering. We must realize that it is in our human nature to avoid conflict, which derives from the classic "flight or fight response." In order to make a real change, however, we must not be afraid to take risks by placing ourselves in the middle of a bullying incident, and having an intervention with the target, bystanders, and bully. Certainly, this type of intervention might be discomforting, to begin with. But this is only in the beginning and will diminish as the intervention continues. This section will give you suggestions on how to have a one-on-one discussion or group intervention with the target, bully, and bystanders.

Intervention Strategies for Bystanders

"You see, but you pretend not to see." — Japanese Expression

Listen carefully and try to validate their experience. Remain unbiased. Don't force your stance, take sides, or criticize any student involved. Ask the bystander(s):

1. Please summarize what you witnessed.
2. How did you feel while watching this occur?
3. What might have stopped you from helping or intervening in this situation? What could you do differently next time?
4. How might you feel now if you did this?
5. How would you feel if you were the target?

---

[2] Pepler, D. & Craig, W. (2000). Making a difference in bullying (Report #60). Ontario: LaMarsh Centre for Research on Violence and Conflict Resolution and Queen's University.

6. How can you help the target feel better today after what just happened?

"In the majority of cases, bullying stops within 10 seconds when peers intervene or do not support bullying behavior."[3]

<u>Words of Empowerment for Bystanders:</u>

- By standing around watching or doing nothing to help stop bullying, you are allowing it to happen and just as responsible and guilty as the bully.
- Be courageous. Step up, speak up, and be heard. Don't forget, there is power in numbers and people to help support you.
- Imagine if it were you. Wouldn't you want someone to be on your side?
- If you let bullying continue, it will escalate. Be part of the solution. You could be a target of bullying one day and no one might be around to help.

Thank them for coming to you and ask them to come and give you an update in a few days. Let them know that the school takes a very strong stand on such incidents and you will be doing all you can to find a solution. Report the incident to authorities using the "Heads-Up Form." Contact administrators and parents if you are not completely satisfied that the bullying will cease. If you feel that the target might suffer bodily harm, contact the police.

Intervention Strategies for the Target

"There is no gain worth talking about when you are in pain. Let us be proactive and brainstorm helpful solutions."

---

[3] Pepler, D. & Craig, W. (2000). Making a difference in bullying (Report #60). Ontario: LaMarsh Centre for Research on Violence and Conflict Resolution and Queen's University.

Bullying can be a sensitive issue for many children and care must be taken to ensure that discussions about bullying do not cause additional distress to vulnerable students. Listen carefully and empathetically, and try to validate his/her experience. Don't take sides or criticize either student involved. However, ensure that the target understands that you empathize with the pain they are experiencing. Help the student feel calm, comfortable, and confident that you care and will do everything in your power to stop this situation from happening again. Don't force your stance (i.e., do not try to explain what the bullied person could do different—just be a listening ear of support for them).

Here are some things that you can do while talking to the **target:**

1. Take a few deep breaths. Take a few moments before asking them what happened.
2. Then ask, "Would you like some **water or Kleenex?**"
3. Encourage them to tell you about **what happened** only when they are ready to talk about it.
4. Ask the student whether it was **the first time** that this bully has done something like this. If not, ask them to tell you, if they feel comfortable, of the prior instances.
5. Make sure to ask if the student has been **hurt in any way** (physically, sexually or emotionally).
6. Try to talk them through what they think the **bully's intentions** were and why the bully would do such a thing.
7. Probe on **how they felt** when the incident was taking place and how they are feeling right now.
8. Ask them what they think you could **do to support them**.
9. Ask the **following questions** if they haven't been covered in the steps above:
    a. What are some things you can do next time to stand up for yourself if this happens again?
    b. What would you like _____ the bully (or bullies) to know?
    c. What would you like the bystanders to know?
    d. What did you learn from this experience? What did you learn about yourself?

PREVENTING BULLYING:
A Manual For Teachers In Promoting Global Educational Harmony

    e.   What is one good thing that came from this experience?
    f.   Is there anything I can do for you to rectify this situation?
10. **Thank them for confiding in you** and assure them that you are always around to help. Inform them that you will take action and speak with the bully and/or others involved in resolving this situation (i.e., to parents, school authorities, or the police). Encourage them to speak to you immediately if such an incident takes place again. Give them your office hours or email address, if they wish to—or need to—speak to you again. Reaffirm to them that no one deserves to be bullied, that they are loved, and the strong stance that the school takes on such issues.
11. **Build their confidence** by stating that you will take their situation seriously.
12. Record the incident to the appropriate authorities using the **"Heads-Up Form."**
13. **Contact administrators and parents** if you are not completely satisfied that the bullying will cease. If you feel that the target might suffer bodily harm, contact the police.

Empowering Solutions for Targets

1. **Don't ignore the problem.** Speak up for yourself and be assertive.
2. **Stay calm** and do not react aggressively. Smile to show your power and confidence (practice this).
3. **You MUST stand up for yourself.** Look the bully in the eyes and tell them to STOP their abusive behavior.
   For example: Be assertive and speak up for yourself if it happens again. Say, "Excuse me?" or "What did you say?" Just show you NOTICE and won't accept the rudeness. Walk away after you speak up for yourself. You don't owe anyone an explanation.
4. **Do not respond** to abusive texts or emails. Save, block and report them.
5. **Tell someone you trust.** Talk to your parents. Practice responses to bullying at home.
6. **Authorities and the police can help you** if threats become overwhelming and serious.

7. **Stay in sight of adults and peers** as much as possible. Avoid areas where the bully is and stay near teachers or large groups of friends.
8. **Report the incident** to school authorities and the police if it is serious.
9. **Make new friends**, or join a club or team.
10. **Keep busy** and active, and try hard to focus on other things. Change your physical and mental state by doing something you enjoy.
11. **Learn self-defense.**
12. **Surround yourself with positive people** who love and support you.
13. Most bullies are either jealous, angry, on a power trip, or suffering inside. Their suffering from family problems or mental health can be factors to their behavior.
14. **The bullying will stop.** The bullying may hurt for now, but overcoming these tough times will **make you stronger, wiser, and more self-aware in the long run.**
15. **Bullying usually happens to the kindest people** because the bullies think they will not confront them. The target usually possesses some positive quality that the bully is lacking and subconsciously knows they are a good person. Now, it's important that you do, too, and stand up for yourself!

Inspirational Sayings for the Target:

- "Don't let someone's bad attitude ruin your good one."
- Stay positive. Fake it till you make it. And one day, "You will be paid double for your trouble."
- Say: "My future's so bright I need sunglasses!"
- I'm always here for you. Many people are here to help you: your parents, your peers, the police, and school administration. You are not alone. Check out these videos/sites: www.itgetsbetter.org.
- Understand that the bully has anger within and is lashing out at you. No one deserves to be bullied. What do you think?
- Tap into your joy and let everyone see it. Show everyone that this won't bother you. Practice with me now. What does a confident person look like?

PREVENTING BULLYING:
A Manual For Teachers In Promoting Global Educational Harmony

Food for Thought Before Your 1-1 Intervention with the Bully

A. *What are some possible reasons why he or she is misbehaving?*
    1. Are they trying to escape work they cannot do?
    2. Are they trying to obtain the attention of the teacher or peers (i.e., class clown)?
    3. Are they trying to gain control over others in order to make themselves feel superior?
    4. Are they reacting to a personal stressor in their home or school environment?

B. *What are possible influences on their aggressive behavior?*
    1. Family structure (internal conflicts, single parenting, poor parenting models)
    2. Relationships (breakups)
    3. Work (unemployment) or school environment
    4. Health conditions
    5. Psychiatric or mental health issues (depression, anxiety, bipolar disorder or PTSD)
    6. Life (or financial) issues
    7. Narcotics
    8. Exposure to violence in the media

Intervention Strategies for the Bully

> *"Don't hit anything harder than it needs to be hit. Use the minimal necessary force to prevent recidivism."* — Dr. Jordan Peterson

Remember that when confronting a bully, that person will likely be very defensive. You need to be patient and let them narrate their side of the story and why they were possibly provoked to do what they did. Remain unbiased. Don't force your stance not to take sides or criticize either student involved.

Here are some things that you can do while talking to the **BULLY**:

1. **Remain calm and in control** when confronting the bully. Explain to them, in an unbiased manner, what they are being accused of and make sure they understand the seriousness of the situation.
2. **Diffuse the situation** if the bully gets too defensive and emotional. Explain to them that you are interested in finding out what happened from everyone's perspective and will not pass judgment on them.
3. Continue by encouraging them to tell you about **what happened**, when they are ready to talk about it.
4. Try to talk them through what their **intentions** were, and why they felt the need to do such a thing.
5. Present the bully with the **"Student Misconduct Reflection Sheet"** and instruct them to take their time and think it through carefully while completing it. After completion of the worksheet, take some time to **review their responses on your own**. After you feel like you have understood the situation and their possible motivation, set aside some time to have a one-on-one discussion with the bully in detail.
6. **Engage the bully in discussing how they think the situation can be resolved.** The aim is to have the bully "on board" and cooperative. Inform them that they have participated in the formulation of a list of sanctions and consequences that all students will all abide by if future bullying incidents occur.
7. Explain to the bully that you are there to help them through this and find a resolution that works for all. The outcome is that the **bully understands and agrees with what he or she must do to atone** for their misbehavior.

1-1 Discussion Questions for theBully

"Aggressiveness happens when someone stops caring about others and lets their frustration get the best of them."

1. Have you ever been bullied? Have you ever been hurt by someone? How did you feel when this person hurt you?

2. What does respect and acceptance of others look like to you? Do you think your attitude or behavior today was respectful?
3. What can respect look like towards this person? What are some nice or polite things you can do?
4. What was the purpose of your actions? What reaction were you hoping for?
5. How do you think (target's name) feels now? How does that make you feel?
6. What will your parents say when I call them tonight and tell them about what happened?
7. What is a logical consequence for your actions?
8. On a scale from 0 to 10, how much did you intend to hurt the target? (0 being not at all, 10 being your sole intention was to hurt the target.)
9. Do you think this situation was funny or acceptable? What was not funny/acceptable about this situation?
10. What did you learn from this experience? Will you behave like this again? How do you feel right now? How will you feel and act tomorrow when you see this person?
11. What could you do now to (a) fix the situation and (b) make them feel better (e.g., apologize and vow never to do it again.)?
12. Is it possible for you to apologize to them?

***Always leave them a way out, enabling a sense of safety ... because that way your message will go deeper into their heart, vs. fighting your resistance of forcing them to do something that is beyond their will and will never result in behavior modification.

N.B. The ultimate cure for bullying is increasing the bully's self-esteem (i.e., self-love and acceptance). Helping the student to value his or her self and to recognize their own inherent potential to do good for others. If we are truly happy, we don't bully others. Do not let the bully leave unless they have understood that their actions are wrong. Make sure that the situation has been rectified and that they sincerely apologize (to the target and the entire class) for their inappropriate actions.

When YOU, the Teacher, is a Target of Bullying

"One teacher in three claims to have been bullied at work."[4]

Quite often, teachers know who the class bully is because of the way he or she interacts with or treats the teacher. There are several well-known cases of teachers becoming targets and experiencing high emotional distress over teaching the class due to one or two disruptive/disrespectful students. This, in turn, usually affects the teacher's overall attitude and ability to teach effectively, putting the entire class in jeopardy of a poor learning experience. One bad apple doesn't have to spoil the whole bunch. Stay true to yourself and act as an authoritative figure, standing up for your beliefs and not tolerating disrespectful language or behaviors.

Bullying in the staffroom is another common form of bullying that teachers experience and can have a deeply traumatic effect on them. The research found that teachers who are victims of bullying suffered: headaches, nausea, palpitations, and hypertension arising from stress. They also suffered psychological effects such as depression and suicidal thoughts.

How to Confront Your Bully

Here are some steps if this happens to you:

Step 1: Don't show weakness. **BE STRONG** and **AUTHORITATIVE**. You are in power as the teacher, and you must take control of your students. If not, they will try to control you and the classroom.

Step 2: Do not ignore what happened because they will do it again and test your boundaries.

Step 3: Ask the bully to see you after class or take them outside of the classroom in that moment to ask them about what their situation is in order to put a stop to their attitude or behavior.

---
[4] Retrieved online (Oct. 2015) from: https://www.highbeam.com/ doc/1G1-197682649.html

Step 4: Make sure they understand that their actions are unacceptable, distracting, and disrespectful.

Step 5: Build a connection and get their commitment to stop their behavior.

Step 6: Make sure they understand the consequences and sanctions of their behavior such as written and verbal apology, push-ups, cleaning the classroom, or detention (optional: meditation for 30 min in silence) and get administrative support and approval. *

How to begin your 1-1 discussion with your bully:

Start with some small talk, and proceed using the following suggestions:

Remember, most students seek attention because they want it. Therefore, they want to be heard and loved because something is usually going on at a deeper level.

Ask questions about his/her personal life:

   a. How are you?
   b. I'm sorry for being so busy and not getting to know you better, but sometimes with so many students, it's hard to keep up.
   c. How are things at home? Is anything bothering you? Are you distracted by something?
   d. Is everything okay with your friends? You seem bothered and angry these days according to your attitude and/or behavior.

Go Deeper. Share your feelings.

   a. Do you know why I asked you to be here?
   b. Share how you feel or what you're noticing: "I feel like you are constantly attacking me / contradicting me / insulting my teaching method / interrupting my class / giving me bad looks / laughing at me / talking behind my back / etc."

c. State the *outcome*: "It's difficult to teach and distracting for me and others. I am here to teach you something and you are disrupting everyone's learning, including your own."
d. Ask: "Are you having trouble in this class? What is your opinion on this subject?"
e. Ask: "How do you think others perceive you when you do this? Do you think you are being funny, a leader, or distracting others from learning?"
f. State the *solutions/options*: "What will you need to be able to focus more in class and not interrupt me while I teach and others learn?"
g. State: "My classroom is a place of learning and if you don't want to learn or be here, then you must leave. But I think you can learn something from this class that will surely benefit you in the future." Give examples.
h. Have the student complete the *"Student Misconduct & Reflection Sheet"* and get signature from parents by next class or they cannot enter.

Give them their **last warning** and note the potential consequences.

Logical Consequences:

a. Write a letter of apology.
b. Notify parents.
c. Apologize to the entire class for disrupting their learning.
d. Write a paper on the uncivilized/unacceptable behavior and why it is wrong and what he or she will do to rectify the situation.
e. Have a parent and the principal intervene.
f. Refuse them from attending your classes if they do not learn to cooperate.
g. Get a school detention or be expelled.

"Be fully grounded in who you are. This is a temporary passing phase. Time will allow you to heal yourself on your own. The law of karma will take care of itself." —Raju Ramanathan

PREVENTING BULLYING:
A Manual For Teachers In Promoting Global Educational Harmony

Do YOU bully your students?

"You will never amount to anything." "Why can't you understand this?" "What's wrong with you?" These are some examples of what teachers may say that can either make or break a student's success in a subject. Teachers, you are their role models, and students mimic teachers' language and behaviors. As educators, it is essential that we reflect on our teaching approach and ourselves. Are you someone who subconsciously bullies your students? Do you play favorites? Do you laugh at or criticize students in public if you disagree with their behavior, beliefs, or attitudes?

Here are some questions to ask yourself when questioning whether you are a teacher who bullies your students:

- Have I ever made fun of a student? If so, why did I do that?
- Have I ever, wittingly or unwittingly, embarrassed or humiliated a student? How and why did I do this?
- Have I ever talked down to or used my authority in a negative manner over a student?
- Have I openly ridiculed any student for belonging to a different religion, race, or orientation?

If you answered "Yes" to any of the questions above, ask yourself these important questions:

1. What could I have done differently? How will I act in the future with this student?
2. What is it about this student that "gets" under my skin?
3. What can I do to rectify the situation?
4. How can I make everyone feel more at peace about our "disagreement?"
5. How can I connect more to this student and make amends?
6. How is this student making me into a better person or teacher?

SECTION 5
BULLYING PREVENTION CLASS ACTIVITIES

PREVENTING BULLYING:
A Manual For Teachers In Promoting Global Educational Harmony

Step 1: Set a Harmonious Tone in the Classroom

Setting the tone of the classroom is critical before talking about something as important and sensitive as bullying prevention. Therefore, at the beginning stages of the program, educators need to ensure that students feel safe, calm, and comfortable in knowing that whatever they say, think, or have experienced/are experiencing are completely normal. Our goal is for students to feel at peace and accepted for who they are in addition to respecting others during the learning process. Simple relaxation techniques, positive affirmations, group discussions about trust, and active listening while setting ground rules will pave the way for an open and compassionate forum about bullying.

> *"Whenever you are teaching, it's important to find out what your students want. The second thing to find out is what they really want. And the third, is to find out what they Really Really Want. Until this is understood, you are not ready to enter the classroom.*
>
> *What are the four fundamental needs we should give our students?*
>
> *Number 1, we need to give them peace and silence.*
>
> *Number 2, the tools on how to make friends. Number 3, the need to develop an eye for appreciating beauty. And 4, the confidence to stand on their own two feet.*
>
> *As a teacher, you need to be living in all these dimensions yourself. No matter what you are teaching, it is up to you to empower them and make your class interesting enough, so bullying does not occur."* — Raju Ramanathan

Activity #1: Create Calmness and Concentration Using Mindful Meditation

> *"Meditation is not a way of making your mind quiet. It is a way of entering into the quiet that is already there, buried under the 50,000 thoughts the average person thinks every day."* — Deepak Chopra

<u>Activity goal:</u> To help students relax and ease their stress while preparing them mentally and emotionally for the subject matter. Numerous studies have proven that deep breathing techniques help prevent stress, anxiety and other related diseases, while also helping increase one's concentration and self-awareness.

<u>Approximate activity time:</u> 15 minutes

<u>Step-by-step activity process:</u>

1. Explain to students that you will begin a meditation session that will help calm the mind and emotions before learning about your subject matter.
2. Note the benefits of meditation[5]:
    - *Rise in IQ and academic achievement*
    - *Reduction of stress, anxiety, and cardiovascular disorders (i.e., high blood pressure)*
    - *Improved concentration and focus (helping those with ADHD)*
    - *Improved and balanced mood and reduction of depression*
    - *Reduction in destructive addictions (i.e., drugs, alcohol, cigarettes)*
    - *Lower level of absenteeism and improved social behaviors*
    - *Increased confidence and emotional stability*

---

5 Retrieved online from: http://tmhome.com/benefits/10-benefits-of-meditation-for-students/

3. Read the following meditation script.

Meditation Script:

- Begin by sitting up straight with both feet on the floor.
- Gently place your hands on your upper thighs in a comfortable and balanced position.
- Make sure your spine is straight for your breath to easily flow through you.
- Now relax your belly and your shoulders.
- Softly close your eyes and start to clear your mind from any scattering thoughts.
- Slowly begin to inhale deeply from your nostrils and exhale slowly from your mouth.
- Breathe in deeply and exhale slowly. (Repeat 3 times.)
- Pay attention to the outside noises, acknowledge them, and let them go.
- Try to be very still and silent. This is one of our goals.
- Next, pay attention to the area around the crown of your head and imagine a calming light flowing down the right hemisphere of your brain, the left hemisphere, the back of your head, and the front of your face.
- Relax your forehead. Let any tension or worries melt away.
- Relax your right cheek, and now your left cheek.
- Relax your nose, your upper lip, your lower lip, and your jaw.
- Now let this light/energy flow down the front and back of your neck all the way down to your shoulders, releasing any tension.
- Let this soothing light/energy flow all the way down your right arm and all the way down to your fingertips.
- Now, all the way down your left arm and all the way down to your fingertips.
- Take another deep breath from your nostrils and exhale slowly through your nose.
- Pay attention to the cool air coming in and the warm air coming out.

- Breathe in deeply again, paying attention to your belly rising as you inhale and dropping as you exhale.
- Feel the sense of peace and calmness running down your body as you bring the energy down the back of your spine, all the way to your hips, and all the way down your right leg to your toes.
- Now, bring this energy down the front of your body all the way down to your left hip, and all the way down your left leg until the tips of your toes.
- Now say to yourself, "My arms, back, and legs are completely relaxed. I am at peace and I am calm. I am filled with love and positivity. I respect myself. I respect and accept others. My mind is relaxed, and I am ready to learn. I feel great and full of joy and gratitude."
- Inhale deeply once more and bring healing oxygen to your body.
- Smile from within and imagine this light pouring out of you from every cell in your body. Expand this light a little more and begin to wiggle your toes and fingers as you prepare yourself to gently open your eyes and bring yourself back to room consciousness.
- Gently open your eyes as you look down, pause for a moment, and then gently close your eyes again.
- Take a deep peaceful breath and open your eyes again, now present and prepared to learn with an open and non-judgmental heart and a clear, calm mind.

Post-activity discussion questions:

1. How would you describe your experience?
2. How do you feel now after this guided meditation?
3. Please summarize the benefits of meditation.

Key take-away message:

The benefits of simple guided meditation sessions for students are ten-fold. With daily or weekly practice, you will certainly see improvements in your students' emotional wellbeing and academic achievements.

Activity #2: Stretch and Feel Great

Activity goal: To help students feel more relaxed and prepared mentally/physically for the subject matter.

Approximate activity time: 10 minutes

Step-by-step activity process:

1. Introduce the session by letting students know the purpose of this activity, which is to help them feel more balanced, focused, and relaxed.
2. Note the other benefits of deep stretching:

    - *Helps reduce stress and anxiety in students' personal and academic lives.*
    - *Helps clear the mind and focus inward, improving one's concentration and preparation for exams.*
    - *Improves students' flexibility, posture, and core strength.*
    - *Activates blood circulation known to prevent diseases while reducing physical pain.*
    - *Acts as a non-competitive activity, leaving students feeling refreshed and with a greater sense of self-acceptance and awareness.*

3. Ask students to stand up behind their desks or in an open space of the classroom.
4. Play some relaxing or uplifting music in the background, depending on your preference.
5. Read the following script:

    - Gently close your eyes and stand up straight. Try to be completely still.
    - Let your head find its center position by using your nose as a guide to align yourself.
    - Take a calming breath by inhaling deeply through your nose, and exhaling from your nose, as slow and smoothly as you can.

- Let's take another deep calming breath. Inhale and exhale, very slowly. (x3 breaths)
- Gently drop your head down to your neck and slowly begin to rotate your head three times to the right (clockwise). Once you are done, go very slowly three times to your right (counterclockwise).
- Concentrate on making full rotations and breathing into the areas where you feel stiffness.
- Once you are done, come back to the center with your eyes closed and your head down.
- Inhale through your nose and you carefully raise your head back to the center.
- Next, rotate your shoulders five times backwards. Make full circles. Inhale as you go up and exhale as you move your shoulders down.
- Once you are done with all rotations, do the same thing going forward. Five full rotations pushing your shoulders forward.
- Next, open your feet apart in alignment with your shoulders.
- Extend your arms out parallel with your shoulders, palms facing the ground, and make five small circles with your fingers.
- Next, with your arms still pointing straight out, turn your torso to the left and point your right hand to the front of your body, looking back behind you to the left, and your left arm pushing as far back as possible. Hold and breathe for 3-5 seconds. This is a great stretch for your spine.
- Return to the center and now change sides, bringing your left arm to the front, stretching your right arm behind you, and looking back towards the right. Hold for 3-5 seconds.
- Come back to the center, slowly bring your arms down, and breathe deeply.
- Next, place your hands on your waist and stretch to the right side of your body, keeping your chest open and stretching yourself to the side as much as possible. Hold for 3 seconds. Now do the same thing on the left side and hold for 3 seconds.
- Come back straight up to the center with your hands still on your hips and slowly bend forward.

- Drop your hands down, almost touching the floor, and stay there for 3-5 seconds breathing gently.
- Slowly roll back up to the center position, feeling each vertebra, reinforcing slow movements not to injure yourself.
- Next, bend your right leg to the back of your body, holding your ankle and using your desk or chair for support with your left hand. Hold and breathe for 3-5 seconds. Repeat this with the left leg.
- Raise your right knee up and rotate your right ankle in a clockwise and counterclockwise direction five times.
- Add in wrists rotations and with some finger bends/curling from the outside moving inward toward the palm and thumb.
- Next, stand up straight, stretching your arms upward toward the ceiling, then pointing slightly backward, curving your back, looking as far back as you could behind you. Hold for 3-5 seconds, and then return to the center position, putting your hands together in the prayer position.
- Pull up towards the ceiling, and then stretch again to the right and left side, holding for 3 seconds.
- Slowly release your arms down to your side, take a deep breath, and relax.
- Inhale deeply while bringing your arms up above your head, hands into a prayer position, aligning each finger, then slowly bring them down to your heart.
- Repeat three times with your eyes closed.
- Open your eyes and quietly sit back down in your chairs with your back straight, mind clear, ready, and focused. Breathing peacefully and joyfully with a smile on your face and ready to learn.

Post-activity discussion questions:

1. How do you feel now on a scale of 1-10?
2. Do you feel more energized and centered?
3. Are you ready to learn something new?
4. Are you ready to focus and concentrate on our next lesson?

Key take-away message:

Everyone benefits from doing simple stretching and breathing techniques. This helps circulate blood flow and oxygen to your brain, and brings a sense of calmness and peace from our chaotic lifestyles. This exercise can be done daily in order to have students center themselves, feel rejuvenated, and mentally and emotionally prepared to learn.

Activity #3: Promote Respect for Self and Others Using the "I Am Mantra"

"Affirmations is anything we think to say and conscious choosing to think certain thoughts that will create positive results in the future and in the now. You are planting seeds for future prosperity." — Louise L. Hay

Activity Goal: To have students say positive affirmations in the present tense and confidently repeat the "I Am Mantra" provided, in order to increase their confidence and respect for self and others.

Approximate activity time: 5-10 minutes

Step-by-step activity process:

1. Introduce the activity by telling students about positive affirmations and their benefits. Inform them that the following activity is intended to help increase their confidence via positive affirmations.

    Positive affirmations *are statements (in the present tense) that you could say out loud or in your head, which help reprogram your subconscious mind to believe that what you say is true. It is like a natural form of self-hypnosis, and it often affects your mood and amplifies positive feelings and actions if done and said correctly.*
    The benefits of using positive affirmations are shown in your increase in confidence, energy level, health, relationships, and overall well-being. If done daily and over time, your negative thoughts will diminish and be replaced with a new, more optimistic way of thinking and living. What you *think* is how you feel and what you will get.

2. Engage your students in a conversation using the following discussion questions:
    - Close your eyes and take 3 deep breaths.
    - Your mind is powerful, and you have total control over it.

- What thoughts could make you feel better now? (Thinking about love, gratitude, good experiences, and your future is an act of loving yourself and creates positivity in your life.
3. Ask students to stand up and repeat the "I Am Mantra" phrases (provided below) after you, in a slow yet passionate tone of voice.
4. Reminder: Pause after reading each phrase, in order to give students some time to reflect and meditate on the meaning, and to reap the benefits.

Extra Option 1: Have students write their own life mantra and read it to the class or in small groups of 4-5 students. Keep in mind that the affirmations must be in the present tense (i.e., I am…).

Extra Option 2: Have students face each other, add gestures, stand up, close their eyes, and repeat the phrases out loud with passion. Copy and distribute the mantra for students to take home or stick to their agendas. Add relaxing yoga or meditation music, and/or mirrors for students to say the mantra to themselves.

I AM MANTRA

I am love.
I am loving.
I am compassionate. I am positive energy.
I am at peace with every breath. I am in love with life.
I am appreciative of all that is around me.
I am grateful for all the wonderful relationships and every single person in my life.
I am grateful for the sun that gives me light and the moon that gives me guidance.
I am so grateful for all my family whose intention is never to hurt me, but to love me.
I am grateful for my past, present, and future teachers who help lift me up when I am uncertain and push me to reach my fullest potential.
I am intelligent and love to learn new things. I am focused and happy, calm and free…
I am strong mentally, physically, and emotionally.
I am healthy, I exercise, stretch, breathe deeply, and drink plenty of water.

I am attractive, unique, and perfect—just the way that I am and was created to be.

I am accepting and loving towards myself and others. I am a true leader when I help and heal others.

I am constantly learning and growing into the person I aim to be. I am my own best friend.

I am in control of my thoughts and feelings today, now, and tomorrow...

I am pushing forward with ease, gentleness, concentration, and awareness. I am filled with joy and gratitude.

I am so grateful for every part of my life! I am so happy to be me.

I love life and I love myself unconditionally.

Post-activity discussion questions:

1. What are positive affirmations?
2. What are the benefits of saying positive affirmations?
3. How do you feel now after saying these phrases?
4. When would it be most helpful to say these phrases? (E.g., every morning to start your day off well.)
5. When do we forget to think this way and why?
6. What are some other ways you can remind yourself to think this way or say these phrases? (E.g., send reminders to yourself using your phone, make post-it notes near your bedside or desk or write in a journal daily of the good things that occur in your life.)

Key take-away message:

Our thoughts create our feelings and experiences, so we must consciously try to think about the right things that are positive and uplifting, which will affect many dimensions of our lives. Life can be difficult and sometimes positive affirmations are needed to keep us strong and on the right path. So, ask your students to think and speak happy thoughts. It's that simple.

Encourage students to come to you if they want to report or talk about a problem they have.

Activity #4: Repeat Positive Incantations

<u>Activity goal:</u> To have students loudly and confidently repeat the following phrases to increase their sense of self, strength, and inner power. You can also ask students to (1) close their eyes while you play soothing music in the background, (2) have them stand up with their hands on their hips (in a power pose), or (3) buy hand mirrors which they can use to look at themselves while saying these incantations.

<u>Approximate activity time:</u> 15 minutes

<u>Materials required:</u> Prize (if awarding); Self-Empowerment statement list (*provided below*) which you can copy onto a PowerPoint slide.

<u>Step-by-step activity process:</u>

1. Tell students that it's important to empower themselves and to say positive things that will help them get through difficult times.
2. Ask students to stand up and repeat the following phrases.
3. *Extra: Have students face each other and add hand gestures.*
4. **If introverted kids seem too shy, ask them to practice alone and have the class clap and encourage with their strong voices.*
5. *Optional: Give a prize to the student who shows the most heart and enthusiasm.*
6. *Extra: Have them close their eyes and shout it out loud.*
7. Read the Self-Empowerment statements (provided below).
8. *Extra: Have students write these motivational phrases in a book or sheet of paper where they can see it. (Recommend sticking it next to their mirror).*
9. Thank the students for their participation.

Self-Empowerment Statements:

1. *I will believe, not doubt. I will create, not follow. I will always love and respect myself.*
2. *I will make positive changes and contributions. I will stand up for others who are bullies or are put down.*
3. *I am fearless, kind, and brave.*
4. *I help others if they are hurt and protect myself if I am hurt.*
5. *I do not judge others according to their race, religion, or sexual orientation. I will judge people based on their character.*
6. *I am wonderful. I am intelligent.*
7. *I can do anything I set my mind to.*
8. *I will never give up. Life is beautiful. Thank you! Thank you, thank you.*
Extra:
Extra:

Post-activity discussion questions:

1. How were you feeling before you said these phrases?
2. How did you feel now, after saying these phrases?
3. What are some ways you can remember these lines in your everyday lives?
4. How can you help others and remind them of these statements?

Key take-away message:

Life is difficult and sometimes some words of hope and inspiration are needed to keep us strong. Students need constant reminders of their self-worth, as this is a challenging and confusing time for them, as well as a critical period in their developmental cycle. Encourage students to come to you if they want to report or talk about a problem they have.

Activity #5: Practice the Art of Listening and Identify Our Human Needs

> *"The Ten Effective Listening Skills are some of the best strategies I ever used. My students instantly became more attentive and I had something to refer to when things got out of hand."* — Diane Ryan

<u>Activity Goal:</u> To help students acquire the "Ten Effective Listening Skills" that will greatly benefit their learning and help educators manage disruptive or disrespectful behavior. Students will identify their own needs in pairs while learning experientially about the "art of uninterrupted listening."

(Part II and III of this activity is suggested for older, more mature students who can grasp these concepts.)

<u>Approximate activity time:</u> 30–45 minutes

<u>Materials required:</u> Flip chart/black board

<u>Step-by-step activity process:</u>

Part I

1. Explain to students that the following activity is aimed at helping them acquire great listening skills. Introduce the class session by asking students:
   a. Is it easy for you to listen to someone without being distracted?
   b. Do you enjoy listening to others?
   c. What are some reasons why being a great listener is important in and outside of the classroom? (E.g., You gain information, clarification, friends, respect, and show compassion, etc.)
2. Ask the class to go into groups of four and brainstorm ways that students can be more attentive in class to increase their learning and attention skills.
3. Once they are complete, ask each group to present their answers.

4. Next, ask students: "What are the best ways to be an effective listener?" Note their answers on the board and ask them how it would improve their learning and academic success.
5. Share the *ten effective listening techniques* (provided below) that can be used to excel in their listening skills in and outside of class, which will benefit their grades and relationships and increase their overall ability to concentrate.
6. Read the *ten effective listening techniques* while students write each technique (in their notebooks or agenda) and discuss examples.
7. Once they are done writing, have the entire class read the ten techniques out loud and process the contents silently.
8. Encourage students to follow these techniques if they want to learn and respect others.
9. Finally, ask students enthusiastically, "Are you ready to be great listeners?"

Ten Great Listening Techniques[6]

1. *Great listeners breathe deeply and feel good.*
2. *Great listeners sit up straight and are mentally prepared to learn.*
3. *Great listeners have an open heart and are accepting of themselves and others.*
4. *Great listeners focus clearly on the topic at hand.*
5. *Great listeners have composed hands and feet.*
6. *Great listeners avoid distractions, including cell phones.*
7. *Great listeners keep their eyes on the person who is speaking.*
8. *Great listeners show politeness by not interrupting the person who is speaking.*
9. *Great listeners are alert and listen from the beginning to the very end.*
10. *Great listeners decide that they want to learn something new.*

---

[6] Adapted from Jane Elliott's Blue-Eyed Brown-Eyed Exercise

Extra:

Make a large poster of the Ten Listening Techniques and hang it somewhere noticeable in class.

Part II: Respecting and Identifying Our Most Basic Human Needs

1. Before practicing the art of listening, tell students that it's important to define our basic human needs, which is essentially it "to be heard" and listened to at times.
2. Introduce the activity by asking students: What are our basic human needs in order to feel good? (Make a list of students' suggestions. Examples: food, shelter, love, acceptance, personal growth, contribution, money.)
3. Ask students, "Which ones are most important for the majority of people?"
4. Next, draw and explain Maslow's Hierarchy of Needs Pyramid (shown below) and review by asking the class:
    a. What are our physiological (physical) needs?
    b. What are our security needs?
    c. What are our social needs?
    d. What are our esteem needs (i.e., ways to feel good about ourselves)?
    e. What are some ways of achieving self-actualization?
    f. What can you do satisfy all these needs for yourselves and others?

Part III: Practicing the Art of Listening

1. Next, tell your students that they will participate in "the art of listening" exercise, where they each take turns listening to their partner's needs *silently* and *without interruption*, because good friends listen carefully and without judgment. Tell them this exercise will also benefit the speaker since they will be able to express their *true needs* and *desires*.

2. Remind students that there is no right or wrong answer; ask them to simply express any need they have and to express it verbally until their turn is over.
3. Next, pair students together with a partner you think they would benefit learning from who is not a close friend of theirs, encouraging new relationships.
4. Ask students to face each other in a secluded area of the room having their knees almost touching each other.
5. Tell students to practice "the art of listening" by repeating the question "What do you need?" to their partner, and then have their partner reply with: "I need..." for 3-to-5-minute periods.
6. Make a note on the board or flip chart that we all have:
    a. Physical needs
    b. Emotional needs
    c. Social needs
7. Make sure that the person asking the question does not interrupt or give their input. They must remain interested and engaged but silent for the person sharing their needs, to ensure a non-interrupted, non-judgmental flow, with free expression and openness.
8. Note that this process is helpful for the person verbalizing their needs. In sharing these needs, they can make certain realizations or connections in different areas of their lives. This process must embody openness and trust for the process to be effective and worthwhile.
9. *Optional: Play background music to set the mood and ensure group privacy.*
10. Once both partners have expressed their needs, have the entire class regroup into a large circle to process the activity.

Post-activity discussion questions:

1. How did you like this exercise?
2. How did you feel sharing your needs?
3. How did you feel while listening to your partner? Was it easy not to interrupt and think of yourself?

4. What need from Maslow's theory do you think is most important for people, after listening to your partner's responses?
5. What deprives us the most from getting these most basic human needs (e.g., your parents, friends, teachers, coaches, negativity, self-doubt, etc.)?
6. If someone is bullied or rejected, how can this affect someone's needs?
7. How could we as a class help each other gain these needs (e.g., showing kindness, respect and sense of belonging)?
8. What did you *learn most about yourself* from this activity?

Key take-away message:

It is important that we encourage participation by making everyone feel comfortable and valued. One way to do this is to practice active listening to show that you are interested in what others have to say. Listen to others, as you would want others to listen to you, with openness and acceptance!

Social belonging is an essential human need where our feelings, ideas, and presence count. Belonging to various groups shapes our social identities, because very often our sense of self is mirrored in others' eyes and reactions. Therefore, when we exclude or reject others, we are taking away one of our most essential human needs. Even if we are different, we all have universal core needs: to be valued, to be loved, and to be accepted.

Optional: Photocopy and distribute to students if needed.

- Needs at the base of the pyramid represent the most basic of human needs (i.e., physical requirements for survival), while those at the top of the pyramid are more psychological and social. These higher-level needs can only be attended to once our basic needs are fulfilled, hence we want to encourage students to help each other feel safe, build friendships, and have a high sense of esteem.

Notes on Maslow's Hierarchy of Needs

There are five basic needs outlined by Abraham Maslow based on the theory that humans are motivated to fulfill their most basic needs first before moving on to satisfying more advanced needs. Therefore, it is important for educators to state our needs, then have students find ways they can help each other achieve some of them (i.e., self-esteem, sense of belonging).

Maslow's Hierarchy of Human Needs:

I. Physiological Needs

The most basic human needs fall into this category. These are the physical requirements necessary for survival, such as the need for water, food, air, sleep, etc. All other needs are secondary to these as humans cannot progress if there is deficiency of these lower-level needs.

II. Security/Safety Needs

Once physiological needs are met, safety and security become a primary concern for humans. This need for safety could manifest in different ways: physical safety (might be amplified during times of war or situations of physical danger such as bullying), financial security (need for steady employment), health safety, etc.

III. Social Needs (Love and Belonging)

This level incorporates interpersonal needs where humans want to feel a sense of belonging and being cared for. Relationships (friendship, romance, etc.) take priority at this level, as does the need to feel part of a society or community, which is especially important for students during adolescence.

IV. Esteem Needs

Once the earlier stated needs are met, humans start looking outwards for appreciation. This is often manifested in a desire for being respected and valued by others (often their peers), which increases student self-esteem.

V. Self-Actualizing Needs

This is the topmost level of our human needs as defined by Maslow. This level represents the ultimate achievement of a person's full potential. This level is defined by everyone's own desires, motivated by their own personal goals and less concerned by the opinions of others. Self-actualizing people are often very self-aware and concerned with their own personal betterment.

Activity #6: Establish Trust — Group Discussion and Action Exercises

> *"You may be deceived if you trust too much, but you will live in torment if you don't trust enough."* —Frank Crane

<u>Activity goal:</u> To encourage students to discuss the meaning of trust in order to help them realize that they should not divulge personal information or those of others with the class. Instead, ask them to seek a professional or counselor's advice. After this discussion is over, students will think about whom they trust the most in class and why, and hopefully model this person's trusting behavior by partaking in the "fall back" and "leading the blind" exercise. (Done with caution, care, and safety.)

<u>Approximate activity time:</u> 15–30 minutes

<u>Materials required:</u> Flip chart/blackboard

<u>Step-by-step activity process:</u>

1. Introduce the session to students as one in which they will talk about and learn how to **trust** one another.
2. Ask students to sit in a large round circle.
3. Open the class dialogue by asking the following questions:
   a. What does trust mean?
   b. Who do you trust most in this world and why?
   c. Who do you trust most in this class and why?
   d. What characteristics does a trusting person have? Do you have these? If not, why not?
   e. Who should you trust about your personal problems or family life?
   f. What would happen if you told someone a secret and they revealed it?

g. Who can you speak to that is 100% trustworthy and will not ruin your reputation or privacy? (E.g., counselor, parent, grandparents, siblings, teacher, coach, police officer, etc.)
h. Why do people enjoy gossiping or criticizing others? (Answer: to feel superior, for humor, or simply to be cruel.)

Activity Briefing:

- Explain to students that we are here to help each other grow and learn, and not to criticize. The exercise will ask them to support and build confidence in each other.
- Tell the class that they are all leaders and should do the right thing and help each other when we fall or make mistakes. So, if someone confides in us or shares something personal in class, we will still "catch" and support them, not gossip or ridicule what they shared. Because we are here to learn, share, and ask questions (but hopefully ones that are not too personal that is meant for a counselor or professional setting).
- Tell students to practice being "trustworthy supporters" and explain that the following two challenges will test their leadership and trustworthiness.
- Ask students to take the challenges seriously as it represents their care and respect for others.

"Falling Back" Trust Activity 1:

1. Make a large open space in the classroom for students to stand in.
2. Have students stand up and divide into two separate lines, with the second line standing behind the first one. (Make sure that students are distributed randomly and not necessarily next to or partnered with their friends.)
3. Tell the students that the person standing behind/in front of them are their partners for this exercise.
4. Next, show the process of letting go and falling into your partner's arms.

5. *Make sure* the person falling back opens their arms completely wide open so the "catcher" can use their arms to catch them beneath their armpits, with their arms steady and strongly stretched out forward. Also have the catcher put one foot forward and stay mentally *focused* on the person who is about to fall back into their arms, ensuring their trust and readiness.
6. Caution students about safety and the importance of not only their own safety but that of their partner as well.

"Leading the Blind" Trust Activity 2:

(*Done with care and caution.)

Materials needed: Blindfolds (If blindfolds aren't unavailable, ask students to simply keep their eyes shut while being led.)

1. Have students get into pairs with someone they do not know very well. Have one person be the leader, who then takes responsibility for leading the other person around the school, hallway, or classroom blindfolded or with their eyes closed. Ask the followers to hold on to the leader's upper arm above the elbow, and stand close beside them, in order to be guided and able to hear clear directions.
2. Make sure the leader pays attention to where they are going and does not allow the follower to get injured, or else they will be held responsible.
3. Note that communication is very important, and that the leader must help the follower trust them by explaining clear directions as to where the follower should go. They should walk slowly and be careful of objects on the floor or in their surroundings that may hurt the follower.
4. Once the pairs have both experienced the follower and leader position, ask them to return in a larger group circle to discuss their experiences.

PREVENTING BULLYING:
A Manual For Teachers In Promoting Global Educational Harmony

"Group Catch" Trust Activity 3: DONE WITH CAUTION

1. Ask 8 students to stand facing each other (4 on each side), with their arms stretched out and grasping the forearms of the person standing directly in front of them (see image below). This will form the "landing pad" for the person falling back.
2. Place a steady chair or table on which the person falling back can stand on.
3. Make sure to appoint someone else as a monitor to ensure that this chair/table remains steady through the exercise.
4. Explain that this exercise is not a joke, and no one will be harmed if everyone pays attention to the person falling back and carries out their role properly.
5. Remind students of the purpose of this activity, which is to demonstrate trust and confidence in each other.
6. Ask for a brave volunteer who wishes to experience "falling back" and trusting members to catch them.
7. Make sure this person is calm and notifies the group before falling back by asking: "Are you ready? 1-2-3, GO!"

Post-activity discussion questions:

1. What did you learn today about trust?
2. Should you trust the class with your personal secrets? Why or why not?
3. What are some things you should keep confidential when discussing bullying prevention?
4. What are some things you feel are okay to discuss?
5. What are the characteristics of a trustworthy person?
6. Are you someone who is trustworthy? Do people trust you with their personal secrets?
7. How did it feel to be led by others blindfolded?
8. What did you learn about yourself from this exercise and discussion?

Key take-away message:

Trust and confidentiality are very important parts of group exercises. People want to feel accepted, not judged. So, if students want to share what you learned, make sure they respect the person and avoid using their name. The story can be just as valuable without a name. Encourage students to keep everyone's personal name inside this classroom. Sharing their names is part of gossiping and intentionally knowing you may be inflicting harm and humiliation. Teens, however, enjoy gossiping at this age so it is important to remind students about the level of trust they should have with their peers regarding their personal or home life. Therefore, remind students to speak with the school counselor when it involves more serious issues that should be left outside the classroom.

Activity #7: Sing and Automatically Feel Uplifted

<u>Activity goal:</u> To sing, contemplate, and unite in the voices by using any of the inspirational songs presented. After a mood of solidarity is set, the teacher can explore students' opinions using the thought-provoking discussion questions. (Extra: Add dance moves.)

<u>Approximate activity time:</u> 20-30 minutes

<u>Materials required:</u> Song lyrics

<u>Step-by-step activity process:</u>

1. Introduce the activity to students by letting them know that they will be singing (and/or dancing) to help promote a feeling of positivity within the classroom.
2. Choose one of the "promoting peace" songs provided (or choose one of your own). Copy the lyrics for each student. (Optional: put the lyrics on overhead from YouTube).
3. Have students listen to the song, then have everyone stand up, clap their hands, and sing along!
4. Next, as a whole class (or in small groups of 3-5), have students discuss and answer the questions provided.
5. Optional: Add fun with dance.
    a. Make random groups of 4-5 students who don't usually hang out together. Have students find a "feel-good or inspirational" song for homework that aims at making everyone feel good and instilling a positive message. Students can present their song to the class by sharing the song's lyrics and singing the song with simple or extravagant dance moves.
       - OR -
    b. Together choose a popular upbeat song that all students agree on. Have groups of 4-5 students come up with their own dance routine in small groups for homework. Optional: have them teach or show the class their moves.

6. Encourage students to just let go and sing (and dance) as though no one is watching, as though it is their last day on earth with their friends and family around them.

Post-activity discussion questions:

1. How did you feel before the song? How do you feel now?
2. How did it feel singing together? What are the benefits? If the dance activity was included, how did it feel to dance together? What are the benefits of dance?
3. What do you think is the main message of this song? What was the singer trying to convey?
4. How does this song relate to your own life?
5. What will you do with the ONE life that you have? How can you help others or promote peace? What can we do as a class project to help stop bullying, racism, and discrimination?
6. What did you learn from this song?
7. What were your favorite lines in the song and why?

Optional Homework Assignment:

Homework: Choose and present a song of your choice.

1. In groups of 2-3, choose your favorite song that relates to the topic of bullying, respect, or compassion for others.
2. On the _____(due date) you must read or play the song (or section) and explain the moral, message or meaning related to the given topic and why you chose this song.
3. Grade: _____%

PREVENTING BULLYING:
A Manual For Teachers In Promoting Global Educational Harmony

Key take-away message:

Music often has a positive, uplifting effect on our mood and causes us to experience greater enjoyment. When we listen to music, we can find a deeper motivation to grow within. Listening and singing together unites us in voice, spirit, and solidarity. Music brings people together in sharing the wholeness and beauty of life. Therefore, it is recommended to fill your ears with motivation and be in a constant state of positivity and love. Take these songs to heart and be the best, kindest person that you can possibly be. Let's respect one another, no matter what, in this wild, precious thing called life.

Inspirational Songs and Discussion Questions

"One" by U2

Group Discussion Questions:

1. What is your favorite line in this song?

2. What do you think is the main message of this song?

3. How does this song relate to your life?

4. What will you do with the ONE life that you have?

5. What does *"one love"* mean to you?

6. How are we carrying or helping each other in and out of school?

7. What are some ways we can help and carry each other through difficult times?

8. What does *"we gotta do what we should"* mean to you?

9. What do you think you should be doing?

10. Do we treat each other like brothers and sisters? When you look at each other, do you see your brother or sister or only differences?

11. How can we be more like one?

12. How do you feel now after hearing this song?

PREVENTING BULLYING:
A Manual For Teachers In Promoting Global Educational Harmony

"Imagine" by John Lennon

Group Discussion Questions:

1. How do you think the world can live as one? What must we do?
2. Do humans share the world and our wealth?
3. How can students live in peace at our school and avoid being bullied? What must we do to help bring peace to bullies?
4. What do you imagine when you think of a peaceful school?
5. What would the world be like without religion?

Other Encouraging Class Sing-Along Songs:

Cindy Lauper True Colors	(Pop) Inspirational song about being who you really are and friendship
Bob Marley One Love Get Up, Stand Up	(Reggae) About peace and brotherly love A song about justice and human rights
Kate Miller Heidke Caught in the Crowd	(Pop) A song about regret and being a bystander
Blink 182 Adam's Song	(Rock/alternative) About the difficulties of being a teen
Mark Willis Don't Laugh at Me	(Spiritual, country & moving) The theme is not to get pleasure from others' pain
Marie Digby Miss Invisible	(Pop, slow song) A song about a girl feeling invisible, a target of bullying

Superchick Hero	(Rock) A song about preventing suicide and bullying
Michael Jackson Man in the Mirror Earth Song	(Pop) Songs about making changes within yourself to make this world a better place
Whitney Huston Greatest Love of All	(Pop) Song about self-love
The Beatles With a Little Help from My Friends	(Pop) Inspirational song about friendship and helping one another
Black Eyed Peas Where is the Love?	(Pop) Fast-paced song about humanity and how we treat one another

Step 2: Create Respectful Ground Rules

"Everyone needs boundaries to be more loving and compassionate towards each other. Is there a game without rules? No. Rules are there to make the game of life more interesting and safer for everyone.

In students' heart of hearts, they love discipline with a combination of loving playfulness. When students bullying one another, it is because they have become hyperactive and do not know where to direct their energy. As teachers, you need to diffuse this energy with play, singing and positive learning activities." — Raju Ramanathan

Bullying is a delicate subject matter and rarely discussed openly in a group. Therefore, it's essential to create a respectful classroom environment where students feel safe to ask questions, share stories and be completely engaged in open discussion.

When discussing this topic, care must be taken to avoid additional stress for vulnerable students, i.e., those being bullied. Establishing realistic and effective ground rules (e.g., in and out of class conduct) is essential. Students must know what is acceptable and unacceptable with regards to what they say and how they say it within these discussion sessions. They must be made to understand the ramifications of their words and their actions on others.

The most powerful class rules that I have used to transform my classroom are the 3 C's vs. 3 A's:

When we:

1. **C**riticize
2. **C**ondemn
3. **C**omplain

... about ourselves or others (i.e., peers, teachers or parents), WE automatically begin to feel low, negative, bitter, unworthy, and critical about our own lives.

On the other hand, when we:

1. Acknowledge
2. Attention (i.e., Give attention to)
3. Appreciate

... others and ourselves, we will automatically create positive emotions that will fulfill every part of our being.

Here are the six **"Good Listening Skills"** that are extremely useful to **begin** and **manage** each class:

1. Good Listeners have quiet hands, feet, and mouths.
2. Good Listeners avoid distractions, including cell phones.
3. Good Listeners keep their eyes on the person who is talking.
4. Good Listeners do not interrupt the person who is speaking.
5. Good Listeners listen from the beginning to the very end.
6. Good Listeners decide that they want to learn something new.

*****

"Never take a person's dignity: it is worth everything to them, and nothing to you." — Frank Barron

Activity #8: Brainstorm Respectful Do's and Don'ts

<u>Activity goal:</u> Before starting detailed discussions on bullying and the prevention of bullying, it is important for students to set and discuss ground rules for showing respect to and receiving respect from each other. (Extra: Post the list of rules in the classroom or school corridors.)

<u>Approximate activity time</u>: 35–40 minutes

<u>Materials required:</u> Paper, pen/pencils, prints of guidelines provided below, blackboard, and flip chart. (Optional: poster making material.)

Step-by-step activity process:

Part I

1. Explain to students that the activity is intended to help them, as a group, set ground rules for future sessions in order to ensure respect is given and received by everyone.
2. Next, ask students to individually write down:
    a. what respect means to them, i.e., a sentence/phrase/word that describes what respect means.
    b. how they act or show respect to someone.
3. Give students 5–7 minutes to complete writing down their responses.
4. Have students share what they have written down with the rest of the class.
5. Optional: Have each student's definition, word or phrase copied and displayed or a poster and hung in the classroom or school.

For Teacher's Use: Definition of Respect

---

respect noun

1. attitude of deference, admiration, or esteem; regard
2. the state of being honored or esteemed
3. polite or kind regard; consideration: *respect for people's feelings*
4. (often plural) an expression of esteem or regard (especially in the phrase *"pay one's respects"*)

verb (tr)

1. to have an attitude of esteem towards; show or have respect for: *to respect one's elders*
2. to pay proper attention to; not violate: *to respect Swiss neutrality*
3. to show consideration for; treat courteously or kindly

Retrieved from: http://www.thefreedictionary.com/respect.

Part I post-activity discussion questions:

1. Who do we respect (a) the most and (b) least *in society*? Where did we learn this from? Is it accurate?
2. How do *we show respect to others in society*?
3. How do *we show respect to our peers*? Do you show respect to all your peers (in and outside of class)?
4. How do *we disrespect our peers*? What are some examples? What are some of the reasons why we disrespect people?
5. How do you think it *feels to be disrespected*? Imagine if you were poor, disabled, gay or colored. Do you think it's a choice or something that's easy to change?
6. Do we feel more powerful or superior when we disrespect others?
7. Have you ever disrespected someone because they were *different or didn't agree with your way of being*? How did it make you feel? How do you think the other person felt?

8. Has anyone been *disrespected by a peer or someone outside of school?* How did you feel? Do you want to share your story?

Part II: Practices on Showing Respect

1. Divide students into groups of 5–6 students.
2. Ask students to make a list of the **"do's and don'ts"** that all should follow in order to be respectful towards each other (in and outside of school).
3. Provide some examples to students of how to show respect. Classify these by the categories presented below:
    a. **Verbal** — speak kindly and positively to one another.
    b. **Physical** — touch each other appropriately and in a friendly, gentle, and caring manner.
    c. **Mental/Emotional** — think kindheartedly.
    d. **Online** — write sensibly.
4. Copy, cut and distribute the *"Showing Respect Guidelines"* papers (see below).
5. Leave students approximately 15 minutes to complete the guidelines, and then ask each group to present their ideas.
6. Optional: Use a board or flip chart to divide students' ideas on how to show respect by verbal, physical, mental/emotional and online categories.
7. Congratulate and thank each group for their ideas, then process the activity with post-activity questions.

Part II post-activity discussion questions:

1. Do you think these respectful guidelines are realistic? (If not, how can these rules be applied in school to prevent disrespectful behaviors and attitudes (e.g., bullying)?
2. Have you ever done any of these do's or don'ts on the list? How do you feel now knowing you might have bullied someone?
3. What are you walking away with from these rules?
4. What did you learn from this activity?

Christina Theophilos, M.Ed. & Raju Ramanathan, M.Tech

<u>Student Guidelines on Establishing a Respectful Class Environment</u>:

1. CONFIDENTIALITY. Do not share the names of students outside of class. You can share what you learned but keep the person's name anonymous. Be respectful.
2. Participate as much as you can and if you're not comfortable, just say so.
3. Try to be open and honest about your feelings or experiences because that is when learning and growth happens.
4. Don't feel obliged to share any personal stories if you're not comfortable.
5. If you don't understand something, ask questions. (There is likely someone who has the same question.)
6. Speak from your point of view. Use "I" statements such as "I feel, think, saw or heard."
7. Don't put other people in the class on the spot by asking them personal questions or name-calling.
8. Acknowledge and respect other people's experiences and opinions.
9. Watch your non-verbal body language: rolling your eyes, looking away or excluding others.
10. Be kind and considerate toward everyone in and outside of class.
11. Respect the confidentiality of everyone in the room and the stories or ideas we share.
12. Try to become closer as a class and trust one another, not put others down to feel better about ourselves.
13. Don't judge each other. Everyone is different with unique experiences, and we should be wise and mature by looking past our differences and instead see the individual for who they really are.

The following table describes a list of *"in and out of class conduct"* behaviors as a reminder to be verbally, emotionally and physically respectful.

If you have nothing nice to say, don't say anything at all!

PREVENTING BULLYING:
A Manual For Teachers In Promoting Global Educational Harmony

Copy, cut and distribute:

<div align="center">*Showing Respect Guidelines:* (Examples: Verbal, physical, emotional, online)</div>	
Do's	Don'ts
1.	1.
2.	2.
3.	3.
4.	4.
5.	5.
6.	6.
7.	7.
8.	8.

Part III

1. Let students know that they will be applying what they have spoken/learned about showing respect to the issue of bullying.
2. Divide students into groups of 5–6 students (or three large groups, if there are too many groups).
3. Assign each group to a type of bullying: (1) Physical, (2) Emotional, and (3) Verbal. Ask them to think about their response to the following question: "What do you think the rules should be about bullying before we start talking about it deeply?"
4. Give students 10 minutes to gather ideas and write their top 5–10 "respectable rules of behavior/code of conduct."

5. *Next, ask each group to present their ideas. (This student presentation section is important since they take authority over their thoughts and become highly involved in the task)
6. Ask other groups to add any suggestions.
7. Make a list or have a volunteer make a list of the class' ideas.
8. Keep the rules on a flip chart and post them in the classroom.
9. Extra: Have students make posters and hang them around the school.
10. Thank students for their openness, efforts, and honesty.

Part III post-activity discussion questions:

1. How do you feel when reading these rules?
2. Are they realistic? Will people follow them? Why or why not?
3. Why do you think setting rules is important? Do you feel more comfortable now that we have set rules to begin our discussion on bullying?
4. What does respect look like? Do you respect everyone in this class? Have you ever broken these rules or bullied someone? Do you only respect your friends or people close to you?
5. What is embarrassment? Have you ever felt embarrassed in class? Give examples.
6. Do you think it's okay to say in class the names of people whom you think are targets of bullying or are bullies? How would that make them feel?
7. Do you think people already know who the bullies and targets are?
8. How are people (i.e., bullies) perceived if they insult/make fun of or share personal stories about others who are here in class (i.e., by looking, pointing, laughing or saying their names)?
9. What is trust? Do you feel that you can trust people in this class? Why or why not?
10. Do you feel comfortable talking about bullying in class? What about with your parents?
11. Do you want to learn more about bullying, its consequences and how to stop it?

12. What would you like to learn about bullying? (TAKE NOTES ON THEIR FEEDBACK.)
13. Are you ready to respect others and the rules, and open yourself to learning? (Say: *Great! Let's get started! Or continue next class!*)

Key take-away message:

Remind students that it is very important to learn how to respect each other and each one's opinion, no matter how different it might be from our own. Note that if respect is not shown, it can cause extreme pain, hurt, humiliation, segregation, violence, etc. To address such a sensitive topic as bullying, one must first create an environment of trust—both inside this classroom session as well as across the school.

Clearly explain to students that if anyone breaks the rules, they will be asked to leave the session and will be reported to the principal/guidance counselor. Remind students that bullying is taken very seriously and each one has a responsibility to prevent it and report it if they witness such a situation. Express to students that with the ground rules for respect laid down, their discussions can be much more open and honest, which in turn will lead to more creative and thoughtful solutions for bullying prevention.

Encourage students to come to you if they want to report or talk about a problem they have. Give them your email or recommend seeing a counselor.

Activity #9: Appropriate Code of Conduct and Sanctions Forms

Activity goal: For students to read, review, and sign their understanding of the types of bullying and associated sanctions. This will act as a type of contract, proving their understanding of bullying and its consequences.

Approximate activity time: 15-20 minutes

Materials required: "Our School's Code of Conduct Form" and "Sanctions for Misconduct Form" (provided). Get two copies of each for each student to sign and return to school authorities and one to keep for themselves.

Step-by-step activity process:

1. It is important to teach this session in an authoritative/assertive manner in order to get the rules across to students about bullying and help define where the lines should be drawn in their behaviors. Bullying is not a laughing matter and neither should be this lesson.
2. Ask students what the 5 types of bullying are and to give examples. (E.g., see form below.)
3. Next, ask students if they know the sanctions (i.e., consequences) to their actions if they bully?
4. Distribute 2 copies of "Our School's Code of Conduct Form" and ask students to read it quietly.
5. Discuss further by asking students to *"raise your hands if"*:
    a. You have ever witnessed one of these types of bullying. What did you do? How did you feel?
    b. You have ever bullied someone else in any of these ways. What was your punishment? How do you think you should have been sanctioned?
    c. You have ever been bullied in one of these ways.
    d. You reported the abuse.
6. Next, ask students if they understand "Our School's Code of Conduct" and whether they have any questions. Proceed by asking students to sign both copies and to return one as a bindingcontract

showing their understanding and agreement that they will NOT bully and will report any incidents they experience or witness.
7. Distribute the "Sanctions for Misconduct Form" and have students read it silently.
8. Ask students what their opinions are of the sanctions and what they think are logical consequences for bullying one of their peers.
9. Read out loud and clarify the ten possible sanctions for misconduct or abuse/bullying.
10. Ask students if they understand all sanctions for bullying and misconduct.
11. Finally, have students sign a form agreeing to the school's guidelines against bullying.
12. Thank students for their participation and collect a copy.

Key take-away message:

Students need to learn what the boundaries are. If not, they will remain in their rebellious state and try to test the limits. Often enough, students don't know there will be consequences to their actions because no one is reporting the abuse or doing anything about it. Therefore, it is especially important that educators let students know that their door is always open and encourage students to come to them, a counselor or a police officer, and they will help stop bullying and make sure consequences are implemented.

BULLYING TYPES	Our School's Code of Conduct Form ALL BULLYING INCIDENTS MUST BE REPORTED
CYBER	I Will Not: 1. Send or display offensive text messages, emails or pictures. 2. Share sexual images of myself or others, which is considered a criminal act and a form of child pornography. 3. Visually record, take pictures and share them with others if they are embarrassing or humiliating. 4. Harass, insult, or use foul language using any form of social media. 5. Spread malicious rumor or gossip online. 6. Send threats or insult someone's character, appearance or behavior using any online media. 7. Damage computers, computer systems or computer networks on school grounds. 8. Use others' passwords or accounts. 9. Hack into others' accounts or personal folders.
SEXUAL	1. Make vulgar sexual comments towards others. 2. Attack someone in a sexual manner. 3. Touch someone (groping) in a sexual manner. 4. Stare/gesture at someone in a sexual manner. 5. Spread rumors about someone's sexual behaviors or identity.

PREVENTING BULLYING:
A Manual For Teachers In Promoting Global Educational Harmony

VERBAL	1. Interrupt when someone else is speaking. 2. Gossip about others or spread rumors that may jeopardize their image or integrity. 3. Call people offensive names. 4. Speak offensively about a certain race, culture or religion. 5. Share a racist, culturally biased or offensive joke. 6. Use homophobic language such as "That's so gay." 7. Use sarcasm that insults or belittles someone. 8. Embarrass someone by teasing them (this is still considered bullying). 9. Scream or yell at someone. 10. Make verbal threats or demands.
PHYSICAL	1. Push, shove, punch, corner, pull hair or pinch anyone. 2. Steal or take anything that does not belong to me. 3. Destroy anything that isn't mine. 4. Use of or showing of any harmful objects/weapons (knives, guns, etc.). 5. Any form of peer pressure to intimidate someone into "fitting in" (e.g., smoking, drinking, doing drugs, etc.).
EMOTIONAL	1. Ignore people when they are speaking. 2. Intentionally exclude my peers from activities or team sports. 3. Give dirty looks (i.e., eye-rolling when someone is speaking). 4. Stare, point, or smirk at someone I do not like.

I _____ (**Print Your Name**) have read and understood our school's guidelines and will see that I follow these rules in order to help prevent any harm to my fellow peers.

Student Signature: _____ Date: _____

Sanctions for Misconduct Form

BULLYING WILL NOT BE TOLERATED. NO EXCEPTIONS. NO EXCUSES.

Sanctions for Misconduct and Abusive Behavior Include:

1. Documentation and reporting of the bullying incident to school authorities.
2. A meeting with the principal and/or counselor involving the harasser, target, and potential bystanders to get each version of the story.
3. Contacting and sharing information with parents or guardians of all parties involved.
4. A written letter of apology from the harasser to the target.
5. A verbal apology to the target (with authority's supervision to ensure sincerity).
6. A public apology from the harasser to the bystanders or anyone else involved to inform them on how they will remedy the situation and what they learned.
7. Appropriate consequences will be determined for the harasser's abusive actions that will atone for their misbehavior
8. A period of detention including specific tasks such as:
   - The harasser writes a paper or letter to the target and his/her parents (1) summarizing the bullying event, (2) explaining their understanding of the negative effects on the target and bystanders, (3) what they could have done otherwise in that situation, and (4) how they *will* or have made the situation better for everyone involved, (5) what they learned from this experience.
9. Assigned community work (i.e., homeless shelters) for the perpetrator to develop a deeper connection with their community and with others.
10. For severe cases of recidivism, more appropriate remediation will be applied, including:
    - detention and counseling with proper authorities.

PREVENTING BULLYING:
A Manual For Teachers In Promoting Global Educational Harmony

- contact with police and law enforcement personnel.
- prohibition on participation in school activities, trips, or sports events.
- family intervention and therapy.
- involvement of local law enforcement.
- expulsion from school.
- anger management classes.

I _____ (**Print Your Name**) have read and understood our school's guidelines and will see that I follow these rules in order to help prevent any harm to my fellow peers.

Student Signature: _____ Date: _____

Activity #10: Establish Class Rules in Small Groups

<u>Activity goal:</u> For students to create their own classroom rules that they believe should be followed and established. In doing so, teachers will prevent disruptive classroom behaviors while enabling students to feel responsible for their own learning.

<u>Approximate activity time:</u> 30–45 minutes

<u>Materials required:</u> Flip chart/black board

<u>Step-by-step activity process:</u>

1. Inform students that the topic for the day is on "establishing classroom rules" that improve our learning environment and promote respect for self and others.
2. Provide a few examples such as:
   - "We close and put our phones away. We come prepared for each class with all our materials. We show respect for the teacher and others by not side talking. We include, support and appreciate everyone in this class with our compassionate words and actions. We treat one another and protect each other like family."
3. Divide students into groups of 4–5 with peers who are not their friends or in the same cliques.
4. Ask them to sit in a circle around a table or desk, which they can write on.
5. Distribute flip chart paper and markers or ask students to take out a blank sheet of paper to write on.
6. Ask students to:
   a. Introduce themselves.
   b. Come up with a funny group name.
   c. Write 5–10 classroom rules. (I.e., Stated in the most positive way.)
   d. State the reasons why they believe these rules are important to follow.
   e. Present their list of rules.

7. Congratulate students for their ideas and efforts for this exercise.
8. State that you have high expectations for them all and know they can achieve these goals, which will better their learning and make everyone glad to be here.
9. Thank them for their cooperation and *commitment* to follow these rules.

Post-activity discussion questions:

1. Can you summarize what the rules are for this classroom?
2. Do you think you can follow all these rules?
3. What are some exceptions to not being able to follow these rules?

Activity #11: Identify Cool and Uncool Behaviors

<u>Activity goal:</u> To have students take a stand on what they perceive to be "cool" or "uncool" by asking them to classify certain statements into these groupings. Students will feel the pressure and necessity of taking a stand while observing the beliefs and reactions of their peers.

<u>Approximate activity time:</u> 30–45 minutes

<u>Materials required:</u> Printouts of "Cool" and "Uncool" labels and statements provided below

<u>Step-by-step activity process:</u>

1. Introduce the activity by letting students know that the activity will gauge what they perceive as being cool or uncool while giving each of them a chance to view how their peers feel about the same thing.
2. Post the "cool/uncool signs" on each side of the wall.
3. Ask students to stand in a single line in the middle of the room so that the signs are on either side of them; ask students to stand at a distance from students on either side so they have space to move around.
4. Give directions to students; tell them that you will be reading out a statement aloud and they will need to move to the side of the room on which they know their respective chosen sign is (e.g., move to the left if a *cool* sign is on the left and corresponds with their answer).
5. Ask students to be as honest as possible because it is the only way to truly learn from each other.
6. Now inform each student that they will be blindfolded. This is to ensure that they do not get influenced by how the rest of the class is moving and that their perception is entirely their own. Once students have picked a side, they will open their blindfolds and see how the rest of the class has chosen.

7. Read the *Cool* and *Uncool* statements one at a time, allowing students time to choose their side, and remove their blindfolds prior to moving to the next statement.
8. Make a note of students' choices (i.e., a rough estimate of how many picked which *cool* or *uncool* by statement), so you can refer to this in the post-activity discussion session.
9. After each statement, probe their beliefs with the following questions:
    a. Have you ever done this?
    b. Do you know anyone who has done this?
    c. What type of bullying is this?
    d. How do you think the target would feel?
    e. How do you think the bully feels in this position?
    f. Is this a realistic occurrence or response?
    g. What would you do if you saw this reaction/behavior?

Post-activity discussion questions:

1. What statement was most meaningful to you?
2. Which statement was most difficult to answer and why?
3. What are some reasons for students' "uncool" behavior?
4. Why do so many people respect or admire bullies who act "uncool" according to this exercise?
5. What have you learned about yourself from this exercise?
6. What have you learned about others?

Key take-away message:

Remind students that everyone wants to be cool, loved and accepted. Hurting someone else intentionally by the way one acts or what one says isn't cool. It is important to respect everyone's feelings. Ask students to imagine themselves in someone's shoes, especially if they are bullying someone or are a witness to bullying. Encourage students to come to you if they want to report or talk about a problem they have.

Christina Theophilos, M.Ed. & Raju Ramanathan, M.Tech

COOL AND UNCOOL STATEMENTS

Note to teachers: When reading these statements make sure to randomize the order so that cool and uncool statements are mixed in the order they appear.

Is it *Cool* or *Uncool* to ...?

Statements	Cool / Uncool
1. Stand up for someone who is being bullied. 2. Tell a counselor or your parents about someone bullying you. 3. Help someone when they get picked on by putting your arms around them and saying, "What's going on here?" or "Are you okay?" "Don't worry, I'm here for you, let's go get help." 4. Use self-defense and fight back to protect yourself. 5. Smile and walk away if you get bullied. 6. Stand up for yourself and tell the bully what they're doing isn't cool. 7. Use humor, and say "I'm not in the mood for a knuckle sandwich." 8. Talk to people you don't know and try to make new friends by asking questions or telling them a joke. 9. Compliment a classmate's skills, talents, personality or appearance. 10. Get to know someone's character and life story before judging them. 11. Respect people of different ethnicities, religions or sexual orientations. 12. Delete unattractive pictures or private videos of you or your friends away from a public forum that can be used against them or humiliate them in the future.	**COOL**

PREVENTING BULLYING:
A Manual For Teachers In Promoting Global Educational Harmony

1. Watch while others are humiliated. 2. Confront or intimidate someone when they're vulnerable while you have more power or popularity. 3. Hit, shove, trip or push someone whom you don't like or have a problem with. 4. Fight using a bat, knife or sharp object. 5. Give attitude or ignore people outside your clique. 6. Leave someone out from sports games, make fun of their skills, then call them a fag. 7. Exclude and think you are better than them because they're different from you (ex: homosexual, different race or religion or style). 8. Call a girl in the school a bitch or a slut because of some rumor or an act that she may have done. 9. Ignore the person harassing you thinking that it will make them stop. 10. Post unattractive or embarrassing pictures, videos of your peers to humiliate them.	**UNCOOL**

CHRISTINA THEOPHILOS, M.ED. & RAJU RAMANATHAN, M.TECH

Copy, cut and paste the signs on each side of the room.

COOL

UNCOOL

PREVENTING BULLYING:
A Manual For Teachers In Promoting Global Educational Harmony

Step 3: Raise Students' Awareness about Bullying

Helping clarify students' awareness about bullying, when it has occurred, and its various forms are essential at this stage. Our objective here is for students to identify their role in bullying as a target, bystander, or bully. Educators must also shift the way students view themselves and the way they think about others, by integrating thought-provoking questions, open discussions, and didactic learning activities.

"Bullying is a misbehavior which is a result of being not cognizant of the two universal truths.

Elizabeth Clare Prophet explains the two universal truths best for educators to consider when teaching bullying prevention. The first truth is, not everyone thinks, feels, acts, or looks like you do. The second truth, is that it's okay that everyone does not think, feel, act or look like you do.

The most important lesson we can teach children at an early age is to enjoy people's differences.

Give people room to be who they are. We are going to meet all kinds of people in this world who do not fit our mold, but more often than not, they have something to teach us. No matter who comes your way, try to keep your heart open and uncover what the universe wants you to learn from them." — Raju Ramanathan

Activity #12: Define Bullying

"A child who is misbehaving is simply a cry for attention. What you perceive as an attack, is a call for love and appreciation."

Activity goal: To have students create their own definitions of bullying in small groups while increasing student/peer understanding, peer group relationships, and teamwork. Often students may not always know that their behavior is bullying, so this activity is a positive way to give examples and help them understand and define bullying.

Approximate activity time: 20–30 minutes

Materials required: None

Step-by-step activity process:

1. Inform students that this activity is intended to help them clearly understand what bullying really means, via examples.
2. Divide the class into groups of 3–5 students (in closed circles, promoting teamwork) in separate areas of the room to ensure privacy and avoid distractions.
3. Tell students to:
    a. Individually brainstorm 3 words that they associate with bullying. (2 minutes)
    b. As a group, discuss what bullying is and create their own definition of bullying, including (a) a few examples of bullying and (b) the effects on the target, bystander, and bully. (15 minutes)
4. Next, ask each group to present their definitions to the class.
5. Then share what bullying is and examples provided.*
    Extra: Make a poster or collage containing all their definitions. Hang the poster in class or somewhere visible in school.
6. Congratulate and thank all students for their participation and efforts.

* See *"useful definitions"* for further bullying description.

PREVENTING BULLYING:
A Manual For Teachers In Promoting Global Educational Harmony

<u>Post-activity discussion questions:</u>

1. How was this task/group assignment? Was it easy or difficult?
2. Did your groups have any problems?
3. Where do you learn about what bullying is?
4. Where is bullying most common?
5. Which group had the best definition and why?
6. Knowing this definition, have you ever witnessed or experienced bullying?
7. At knowing these definitions, raise your hand if you've ever been a bully. (Note that sometimes we aren't aware of our actions and think they are funny or just teasing.)
8. What will you remember most from this activity?
9. Are you more aware of what bullying is now?
10. What will you do if you see someone being bullied? (Answer: Speak up, report it and console the target. No one should go through difficulties alone or be humiliated.)

<u>Key take-away message:</u>

Knowing what bullying is and all its forms are the first step to becoming aware of our actions and the actions of others. Encourage students to put an end to bullying and seek assistance if they ever are a target or bystander. Remind students that there is always help available at school (teacher, counselor, principal, school administrators, etc.); all they need to do is ask for this help.

Helpful Definitions

Bullying can be *direct* or *indirect*.

- *Direct bullying* is when the bully confronts the target face-to-face. Examples of direct bullying involve situations where the target is verbally harassed or threatened, physically attacked (e.g., punched, kicked, pushed down), or socially embarrassed (e.g., teased, excluded, ignored).
- *Indirect bullying* is when the bully attacks the target's reputation when the target is not around. Examples include spreading rumors, gossiping, exclusion, writing insulting graffiti, threats on email or text messages, or organizing a peer group to ostracize that classmate.

The key elements of bullying are:

- the imbalance of power.
- the bully's intent to do harm.
- the target's suffering.
- repetition over time (reputations and power differential become consolidated).

> ➢ "Bullying is to treat abusively and to affect by means of force or coercion and to use browbeating language or behavior." — Webster's Dictionary
> ➢ Laws define "bullying" as any repeated overt acts by a student or group of students directed against another student with the intent to ridicule, humiliate, harass, or intimidate the other student while on school grounds (including on transportation vehicles) or at school-sponsored activities.

PREVENTING BULLYING:
A Manual For Teachers In Promoting Global Educational Harmony

- ➤ Bullying behavior is a form of aggression where someone uses their power repeatedly over time to purposely hurt someone.
- ➤ "Terrorizing, intimidating, shunning, tormenting and ridiculing are not sibling rivalry or peer conflicts. They are acts of bullying."— Barbara Coloroso
- ➤ "The opposite of love is not hate, but indifference; indifference creates evil. Hatred is evil itself. Indifference is what allows evil to be strong, which gives it power."— Sam Durant
- ➤ Bullying is the misuse of power, intended to cause harm. Repeated effects are serious and can cause depressions, anxiety or even suicide.
- ➤ One hundred sixty thousand kids in the US stay home every day because they're afraid of getting bullied. (Source: The Bully, The Bullied, and the Bystander, 2002)

---

1. Because bullies can, if and when no one stops them.
2. Ignorance: They don't realize that their actions are harmful.
3. Bullies think their actions are funny.
4. Bullies seek power, control, and popularity.
5. Bullies seek group admiration and acceptance (even if it goes against their own morals and values).
6. Bullies want to copy/model others they admire who are behaving like bullies or speaking insensitively.
7. Bullies enjoy humiliating and overpowering others.

EXAMPLES OF THE FIVE TYPES OF BULLYING

1. **Cyber/Online Bullying:**
    a. Voting the fattest, ugliest, least popular, or worst dressed person in the class online
    b. Making insulting or sarcastic comments on Facebook or other networks
    c. Tagging humiliating videos or pictures or sending them to other people by phone or email
    d. Sending abusive/nasty/threatening messages on a chat room, instant messenger, or text message
    e. Taking someone's online identity or password and reading their messages (gossiping/invasion of privacy)
    f. Prank calling

2. **Verbal Bullying:**
    a. Name-calling (sometimes seen as teasing)
    b. Harassing them to do or say something
    c. Spreading gossip or lies (rumors)
    d. Insulting one's family, status, or religion
    e. Yelling at someone
    f. Insulting or nagging
    g. Making verbal threats or demands
    h. Making noise as they pass by
    i. Racist jokes

3. **Physical Bullying:**
    a. Making threatening poses (fists, cornering someone)
    b. Stealing their lunch, money, clothing, homework or books
    c. Pushing, punching, pulling hair, flicking or bumping into them on purpose

    d.   Use or showing of weapons (knife, bat, or gun)
    e.   Throwing or hiding their belongings
    f.   Damaging their things
    g.   Spitting or flicking paper, rubber bands or any other object
    h.   Burping in their face

4. Non-verbal Bullying:
    a.   Intentional exclusion from games, sports, conversations, planned activities or parties
    b.   Ignoring the person
    c.   Giving the "silent treatment"
    d.   Whispering and pointing while looking at the target
    e.   Glaring
    f.   Sticking tongue out at them
    g.   Peer pressure to smoke, drink or steal
    h.   Using gestures to intimidate or threaten

5. Emotional/Psychological Bullying:
    a.   Verbal: comments or questions related to sexual orientation (homophobic bullying), gender
    b.   Physical: pinching, groping, touching, looks, whistling
    c.   Racial: comments, jokes, physical abuse or exclusion due to the color of their skin or ethnicity/race
    d.   Religious: comments, jokes, physical abuse or exclusion based on religious beliefs or nationality or community
    e.   Disability: making comments, jokes, physical abuse, or exclusions based on their physical or learning disability (or of their friend or family member)

Activity #13: Class Discussion and Questions About Bullying

(Short & Long Version Included)

Activity goal: To have an open discussion about bullying and emphasize how we must be respectful of everyone's feelings and do no harm. This discussion can act as an icebreaker and give you a sense of the class dynamics, relationships, and basic needs.

Short Version

Recommended if teachers have limited time for other activities.

Approximate activity time: 15 minutes

Materials required: Print of "Bullying Discussion Questions" (depending on selected activity).

Step-by-step activity process:

1. Let students know that the session will allow them an opportunity to openly talk about bullying; clarify any questions and raise any concerns they might have.
    a. Ask students the following questions:
    b. What is the purpose of going to school? (Answer: to learn, grow, mature and have fun.)
    c. What will a good education prepare you for? (Answer: a job, knowledge, everyday life, math, science, English… You need to learn these things even though they may seem useless right now!)
    d. Can students learn/study if they are worried about getting bullied?
    e. Is it easy to study when you're worried about your personal life (e.g., rumors, bad text message or Facebook remark, or a humiliating joke someone just said)?

f.   Raise your hand if you've ever been bullied online, verbally or physically in your life?
g.   How did it feel?
h.   What is bullying exactly? What types of bullying are most common at school?
i.   What are the outcomes of bullying? (*Review: Introduction & Description of Bullying*)
j.   If you could comfort a target of bullying, what would you tell them that you think is most important?
k.   How do you think (a) targets, (b) bystanders and (c) bullies really feel?
l.   Why do people bully even if they know it's wrong? (Answer: power, control, mimicking others, popularity, the release of anger or frustration about something in their lives, unaware/ ignorant.)
m.   What are some things you can do if you are being bullied or witness it?

Long Version

Approximate activity time: 50 minutes

Materials required: None

Step-by-step activity process:

Let students know that the session will allow them an opportunity to openly talk about bullying; clarify any questions and raise any concerns they might have.

Option 1

Read it out loud or copy the "Bullying Discussion Questions" (provided below) on your PPT or overhead to have a large group discussion. (Sitting in a sharing circle where everyone can see each other's facial expressions is recommended. This creates an open place for sharing and personal reflection, building group solidarity versus the typical classroom setting.)

Option 2

Copy "Bullying Discussion Questions" and distribute to each student. Have them answer the questions individually and then further discuss in small groups of 3-5 students.

- Ask students for their attention and to get into a focused/respectful mindset as you begin to talk about the sensitive nature of bullying.
- Encourage participation and honesty because many students experience bullying daily, and we need to work together to solve this problem.
- Tell them that you hope they will remember what they've learned and to report all forms of abuse when they see or experience it.

PREVENTING BULLYING:
A Manual For Teachers In Promoting Global Educational Harmony

Copy, cut and distribute the following questions to each group:

See the version for teachers following these questions.

Bullying Discussion Questions

<u>General Questions:</u>

1. Describe your definition of bullying in one sentence.
2. What are some examples of bullying *in* school?
3. Where does bullying usually happen *in* school?
4. Where does bullying happen *outside* of school?
5. What are some reasons why people bully abuse or harass others?
6. Where do people learn that it's okay/acceptable to bully others?
7. What are some common traits, stereotypes and/or characteristics of people who are *bullies*?
8. What are some common traits, stereotypes, and/or characteristics of people who are *targets* of bullying?
9. If the common target isn't around, who will they bully next?
10. Are people usually around when bullying happens?
11. What is a bystander?
12. Have you ever tried to help a target of bullying by reporting the abuse or consoling the target?
13. What are some common reasons why bystanders don't help defend targets of bullying?
14. If you could be a bully, target, defender/helper or bystander, who would you like to be the most and why?
15. *Who is:*
    a. The most powerful? The bully, target, helper or bystander?
    b. The coolest? The bully, target, helper or bystander?
    c. The smartest? The bully, target, helper or bystander?
    d. The friendliest? The bully, target, helper or bystander?
    e. The most respected? The bully, target, helper or bystander?
    f. The least respected? The bully, target, helper or bystander?

Let's Get Personal:

The bullies ...

16. Do you know any *bullies* at this school? Yes or No? Are there many?
17. How do you act and feel towards them?
18. Do you think it's okay that they bully others? Have you ever tried to stop them from bullying, or report what they do to authorities?
19. Have *you* ever bullied someone in or outside of school? (Share stories.)
20. How do you think the target felt when you did this?
21. How did *you* feel *while* doing it? How did you feel *after*? How do you feel now?

The targets ...

22. Do you know any *targets of bullying* at this school? Are there many?
23. Have you ever been a target of bullying? (Share stories.)
24. What are some general consequences of bullying for the target?
    a. What are some *physical* effects?
    b. What are some *social* effects?
    c. What are some *emotional* effects?
25. What are some realistic ways a *target* of bullying can defend themselves?
26. What are some realistic ways *bystanders* can help?
27. What can the *school* do to help targets of bullying?
28. How can *everyone* in this class make sure bullying doesn't happen in and out of school?

(Write their ideas on the board.)

PREVENTING BULLYING:
A Manual For Teachers In Promoting Global Educational Harmony

Bullying Discussion Questions

-For Teachers' Use Only-

General Questions:

1. Describe bullying in one sentence.
   "Bullying is to treat abusively and to affect by means of force or coercion and to use browbeating language or behavior." — Webster's Dictionary
2. What are some examples of bullying in school?
   - Actions commonly expressed **verbally** (using words), **physically** (angry eyes, shoving), or **psychologically** (relational bullying), which attempt to **exclude**, embarrass or damage the reputation of the target (e.g., gossiping or spreading rumors)
   - **Harassment,** which can be shown by pushing, making intimidating phone calls, laughing while pointing at the target, rejecting/ignoring the target from a circle of friends, commenting on the target's height, weight, dress or appearance and so on
   - Online forms of communication, **cyberbullying** and psychological violence (e.g., hurtful text messages, unattractive tagged photos, sarcastic/ harsh personal comment
3. Where does bullying usually happen in school?
   - Bullying usually happens **away from adult supervision,** since they know sanctions can occur with an adult present. Therefore, bullying is often done **outside of the classroom, in bathrooms or hallways, after school or at lunchtime** or wherever else the target is vulnerable and where witnesses are present.
4. Where does bullying happen *outside* of school?
   - Bus stops, bus, outside school, online, text messages, online forums
5. What are some reasons why people bully, abuse or harass others?
   - Because they can, and no one stops them.
   - Ignorance: They don't realize that their actions are harmful.
   - They think it's funny.

- They seek power, control, and popularity.
- They seek group admiration and acceptance (even if it goes against their own morals and values).
- They want to mimic people they admire or look up to, who are reinforcing bullying behaviors.
- They enjoy humiliating and overpowering others.

6. Where do people learn that it's okay/acceptable to bully others?
   - Parents, siblings, friends, media
7. What are some common traits, stereotypes and/or characteristics of people who are *bullies*?
   - Insecure, popular, angry, tall, big, pretty
8. What are some common traits, stereotypes and/or characteristics of people who are *targets* of bullying?
   - Weak, quiet, shy, insecure, short, different from the norm or majority, smart, introverted
9. If the common target isn't around, who will they bully next?
   - You and anyone else who is "under them" or available to be picked on
10. Are people usually around when bullying happens?
    - Yes, bullies like to be viewed by others to get attention. Adults and teachers are usually not present.
11. What is a bystander?
    - Bystanders or people who **watch** bullying occur are almost always aware that they are doing nothing to help the target and feel their pain or humiliation.
12. Have you ever tried to help a target of bullying by reporting the abuse or consoling the target?
13. What are some common reasons why bystanders don't help defend targets of bullying?
    - They usually are afraid and do nothing to help and feel like they don't want to **"get involved"** because they do not want to be at the center of attention, lose their popularity or reputation or be the next target.
    - Other times, they are being highly influenced by their peers and forget to think morally about what is right and wrong and simply **"follow the crowd"** and laugh when situations

are considered funny, even when they're hurtful. Bystanders, like most teens, seek **acceptance** and a **sense of belonging** and sometimes go against their innate values in order to fit in, oftentimes without even realizing their actions.

STUDENT OPINIONS

14. If you could be a bully, target, defender/helper or bystander, who would you like to be the most and why?
15. Who is:
    - The most powerful? The bully, target, helper or bystander?
    - The coolest? The bully, target, helper or bystander?
    - The smartest? The bully, target, helper or bystander?
    - The friendliest? The bully, target, helper or bystander?
    - The most respected? The bully, target, helper or bystander?
    - The least respected? The bully, target, helper or bystander?

Let's Get Personal:

The bullies...

16. Do you know any *bullies* at this school? Yes or No? Are there many?
17. How do you act and feel towards them?
18. Have you thought that it's okay that they bully others? Have you ever tried to stop them from bullying or report what they do to authority?
19. Have *you* ever bullied someone in or outside of school? (Share stories.)
20. How do you think the target felt when you did this?
21. How did you feel *while* doing it? How did you feel *after*? How do you feel *now*?

The targets...

22. Do you know any *targets of bullying* at this school? Are there many?
23. Have you ever been a target of bullying? (Share stories.)
24. What are some general consequences of bullying for the target?
    - What are some physical effects?
        - <u>Caused by others</u>: bruises, scratches, cuts or ripped/stretched out shirts.
        - <u>Caused by stress</u>: headaches, backaches, stomach aches, bedwetting, loss of hair, skin disorders, sleep difficulties,

nightmares, irregular menstruation, loss of appetite or overeating, pale skin, tense and weak immune system resulting in illnesses.
- <u>Caused by self:</u> smoking, drinking, drug abuse, absenteeism, changing schools, dropping out of high school, cutting and even suicide.

- What are some *social* effects?
  - <u>Peers:</u> They avoid and feel uncomfortable around tense, insecure students (who perhaps remind them of their vulnerability).
  - <u>Friends:</u> They distance themselves from the target and merge with new friends, fearing association with the target or getting bullied themselves. Targets may be attached to one friend to feel secure and not alone. Also, they may stay in a "trendy or secure" group of friends where they are being bullied but would rather stay in it to feel a sense of belonging to that group.
  - <u>Family:</u> Parents feel helpless and inexperienced to help support their child. The target may isolate themselves from family members and avoid burdening or disappointing their parents.
  - <u>Gatherings:</u> Targets may avoid areas where they can be targeted (large crowds, school buses, and cafeteria). As a result of their exclusion and disassociation, they are often not invited to parties, are last to join games or group projects, and have a poor social life.
  - <u>Social skills:</u> Targets become isolated and fear being hurt and rejected again so they often have difficulty making new friends and forget how to trust others.

- What are some *emotional* effects?
  - <u>Shock:</u> Targets are usually shocked and surprised at first but then fear freezes them to do anything about it, while "disaster movies" of the worst-case scenarios and future encounters replay themselves in their heads.
  - <u>Sickening fear:</u> They feel like their world is unsafe from people superior to them.

- <u>Learned helplessness:</u> It is the belief that there is nothing they can do to escape or help their situation.
- <u>Depression and anger:</u> Such emotions are felt towards people they feel comfortable with, like parents, and they fantasize about revenge.
- <u>Identity crisis:</u> Targets forget who they are and their self-worth and begin self-loathing or believing what the bully thinks. They feel undesirable and incapable.
- <u>Hitting Rock Bottom:</u> They can't bear the distress, so they usually find solutions or seek help from others.

25. What are some realistic ways a *target* of bullying can defend themselves?

   What to do if you're being bullied:
   - **Act confident.** Stand up straight, speak clearly, and look secure even if you aren't. Make the person think they are not bothering you and they are wasting their time trying to tease you.
   - **Stay calm; don't say anything nasty or act offended or angry.** This is probably what the person bullying wants you to do.
   - <u>Keep your words simple.</u> Don't get too wordy or emotional. Be assertive, and then walk away. Ignore what the bully will say next to try and get the last word.
   - **Make a joke and say:**
     - "I love you too!"
     - "You're so lovable!"
     - "You're so wonderful!"
     - "Thank you, have a nice day!"
     - "Wow, that was so nice of you!"
   - **Show that you don't care by saying things like:**
     - "I don't really care what you think."
     - "I'm not really interested."
     - "Who cares?"
     - "So?"
   - **Calmly remove yourself from the situation.** Say your piece, then walk away or ignore the bullying by turning and walking away calmly and confidently.

PREVENTING BULLYING:
A Manual For Teachers In Promoting Global Educational Harmony

- **If they try to stop or block you,** be firm and clear—look them in the eye and tell them to stop.
- **Don't fight back.** If you fight back, you could make the situation worse, get hurt, or be blamed for starting the trouble. "An eye for an eye makes everyone blind"— Gandhi.
- **Take a martial arts or self-defense class** if physical abuse continues. You can also study some blocking positions online. Practice with a friend or family member so you can be prepared for an attack.
- **Get away from the situation** as quickly as possible and go cool down somewhere.
- **Go tell an adult** what has happened straight away. **Don't be afraid** to talk to an adult you trust (like your teacher, counselor or your parent). Brainstorm solutions or interventions together. Keep talking to them until the bullying has stopped.
- **Tell a friend about it.** Try to avoid being alone in places the bully may pick on you. Go where there are plenty of people and ask a friend(s) to go with you. Stay or act calm and practice what you can do the next time if the bullying happens again. Remember that bullies usually want a negative reaction from you.
- **Think positively.** Remember you are a good person. Remind yourself of your strengths and the things you are good at and that it will get easier. We all have a purpose in life and these experiences will make us stronger and enable us to help others who have experienced pain.
- **Attend youth or religious centers** (e.g., church, synagogue, mosque or temple, or a youth group where you can talk to people, meet new friends, get support and pray about your situation. This is another effective way to gain strength, wisdom and inner peace.).
- **On the school bus,** try to sit near the driver and talk to the people around you. If it's a city bus, sit close to adults where you feel protected and get off before or after the bullies. If it is still too difficult, talk to the bus driver or ask the school to intervene ASAP.

- **Walking home.** If you have to walk home and you're afraid of being ambushed, try taking different routes, try to leave home and school a bit later or a bit earlier, or see if you can walk with other people who live near you, even if they're older or younger.
- Learn self-defense or take some martial arts classes.

26. What are some realistic ways *bystanders* can help?

    What to do if you're a bystander:
    - **Spread the word** that bullying isn't cool. It won't be long before everyone agrees.
    - **Walk away** instead of standing and watching bullying. Don't encourage it. Go get someone to help (like a nice senior or teacher).
    - **Tell the bully** that their actions are wrong and that they should go see a counselor if they seek attention. Ask them not to take it out on others.
    - **Help the person being bullied** by talking to them and telling them it's going to get better. If you're too shy, write them an email and give them some advice.
    - **Report the incident** to a parent, teacher or counselor ASAP.
    - **Refuse to hang out with people** who are mean to others. Show people that it's not cool to be disrespectful and you do not want to be part of it.
    - **Interrupt the abuse** by saying "STOP!" or "Get away from them!"
    - **Be a leader, be a friend.** Don't be afraid. Make a stand. Remember your values. Imagine it was you. What would you want someone to do to help you?

27. What can the *school* do to help targets of bullying?
    - Contact the bully's parents and have an intervention.
    - Contact the target's parents.
    - Have more severe and logical consequences for the bully to follow if he or she has bullied another student. (E.g., public apology, refrain from having recess with others, etc.)
    - Have the target and bully together and discuss the issue with a third party who can make the bully understand that

their actions are wrong and hurtful and not leave the room until it's clearly understood.
- Talk to the whole class about reporting bullying and ways to stop it together.
- Use class prevention exercises and lectures in each class and grade for a comprehensive understanding.
- Put higher punishment for students who bully (in and out of school) and a zero-tolerance policy.
- Promote acts of kindness.
- Have a school play, an anti-bullying campaign or guest speakers talk about their bullying experiences and how they overcame it. The bullying will eventually stop, but you must defend and speak up for yourself using an authoritative voice!

28. How can *everyone* in this class make sure bullying doesn't happen in and out of school?
    - Step up and stop bullying if you witness it.
    - Report someone's behavior if it's bullying.
    - Comfort and defend the target.
    - There is power in numbers. Make a positive change together. You are not alone.
    - Promote respect and acts of kindness. Spread love, not hatred.
    - Watch your words. Speak nicely to one another. Don't criticize, gossip or judge one another.
    - Be mindful of your attitude and behavior. Make sure it's loving, not aggressive or overpowering.

Post-activity discussion questions:

1. How do you feel now after these questions?
2. What questions were most difficult for you to answer?
3. What will you remember most from this discussion?
4. What did you learn today?
5. What could you do if you ever get bullied?
6. What can you do if someone else is getting bullied in front of you?

Key take-away message:

Bullying should not be tolerated or thought of as funny, just a joke or normal. It's wrong, hurtful, and can ruin someone's entire school life. Everyone is involved and responsible. There are no innocent bystanders. Bullying must stop and be reported so action can be made against the bully for them to learn that their actions are not tolerated in school or society. Life is too short to live in pain. Let's promise to work together and protect each other.

Activity #14: Bullying Word Associations — Icebreaker

Part 1:

Activity goal: To have students express a word or two that describes their thoughts or feelings about bullying, which can be used as an icebreaker activity.

Approximate activity time: 10–15 minutes

Materials required: Flip chart/blackboard, marker

Step-by-step activity process:

1. Let students know that they will be playing an ice-breaker game to initiate future discussions around bullying. Tell students that we all have different words associations to express our emotions or opinions about bullying. So, this activity will give us a chance to hear everyone's brief perspectives.
2. Have students sit or stand in a circle.
3. On a flipchart or blackboard, write down the four words listed below, i.e., Bully, Target, Bystander, and Helper.
4. Next, have students say the first word that comes to their mind that expresses the way they think or feel when they hear the word:
   a. **Bully** (e.g., powerful, crazy, strong, scary, mean, funny)
   b. **Target of bullying** (e.g., weak, pity, afraid, loner, excluded, victim, pain)
   c. **Bystander** (e.g., scared, unsure, coward)
   d. **Helper/defender** (e.g., brave, leader, confident, caring)
5. For each "topic," write down the word associations below the title.
6. Probe students if certain word associations are not clear; ask them to explain why they picked that word.
7. Thank the students for their participation.

Post-activity discussion questions:

1. What word was most difficult to answer for you and why?
2. What word was easiest to answer and why?
3. Do you think your reaction to the words have something to do with your role and behavior in bullying?
4. Did any specific word association(s) surprise or bother you?

Key take-away message:

Everyone has different opinions about bullying and our words express our true feelings. Therefore, it's helpful to know the power of words and how they can evoke strong emotions. Words and word associations are different for everyone according to our experience with them, so what we might think is harmless may be insensitive or hurtful to others.

Part 2: Understanding E.M.P.A.T.H.Y.

Activity goal: The aim of this activity is to encourage empathy, build teamwork and promote creativity among students in finding solutions for those students who are being bullied or socially excluded.

Approximate activity time: 15–20 minutes

Materials required: Empathy Worksheet provided, pens/pencils

Step-by-step activity process:

1. Introduce the session to students by informing them that they will be learning about empathy for each other via exercise.
2. Divide students into groups of 4 to 7.
3. Ask students to share a personal experience of a time they felt empathy for someone at school, in their family, or in the community. Tell them to explain the situation and why they felt empathy.

4. Have students work in their groups to come up with an acronym using EMPATHY in order to stop bullying in and outside of school. (Use the Student Worksheet provided below.)
5. Once each group has completed their acronym, ask them to share it with the rest of the class.

Post-activity discussion questions:

1. Why is it important to feel empathy for others?
2. What benefits does empathy have on society as a whole?
3. How does one know when to show compassion towards another person?
4. For whom do you feel the most empathy and compassion and why?
5. Should the greatest love be towards others or ourselves?
6. What does it mean to love and accept ourselves?
7. Why do some people feel more empathy while others feel very little?
8. How does empathy relate to bullying?

Key take-away message:

Empathy is usually experienced and related to your own personal life experience of seeing others close to you in pain or suffering. It is also inspired by how those around you have shown empathy towards your own personal trials and tribulations. There are many positive aspects from showing empathy and compassion towards others, such as a greater sense of self-awareness and letting the other person know they are not alone and cared for, which everyone needs. Empathy can be so simple, such as a confirming glance or smile from a stranger across the room that implies, "I know what you're going through."

"**Empathy:** the feeling that you understand and share another person's experiences and emotions: the ability to share someone else's feelings."— Merriam-Webster Dictionary

CHRISTINA THEOPHILOS, M.ED. & RAJU RAMANATHAN, M.TECH

Student Worksheet

What is EMPATHY?

What is COMPASSION?

Activity #15: Demystify Bullying — True or False Exercise

Activity goal: For students to understand the myths and truths about bullying by answering a set of "True or False" discussion questions. This activity provides a few different options (to either perform as one large class or divide into smaller groups to encourage small team interactions), and it is left to the discretion of the educator which one to choose, depending on what would be most beneficial for their class.

Approximate activity time: 30 minutes

Materials required: Printouts of True/False signs, copies of *"True or False Bullying Statements"*

Step-by-step activity process:

Option 1 — This activity is extremely effective for students to take a stand on their positions and beliefs about bullying via answering True/False statements.

1. Move the desks of the class to provide lots of space for students to move from one side to another. Ask students to clear an open space for students to walk on either side of the classroom.
2. Copy and paste the signs to each side of the room. (Useful size version attached — see below)
3. Tell students that they are going to play a "true or false" activity related to bullying in order to help understand their values and behaviors of bullying.
4. Next, ask students to stand up and move to the side of the wall that pertains to their answer.
5. Note that honesty is the most important element of this exercise. Without it, there is no growth or real learning.
6. Begin reading the "True or False Bullying Statements" and consult the provided teacher's responses.
7. Encourage students to share their stories or opinions and thank them afterward.

Option 2 — This activity gauges students' awareness of bullying via a True or False exercise. It is interactive and very powerful if done with care.

1. Copy, cut and distribute a small "True or False" box to each student (except the *moderator*).
2. Have students form 2–3 large groups depending on your class size or preference (6+ students per group is preferable). Have each group sit in a tight circle or square.
3. Distribute one copy of the *"True or False Bullying Statements"* sheet to each group (face down).
4. Select a moderator for each group who will:
    a. read the questions and remain neutral.
    b. make sure everyone listens and has time to respond to each statement.
    c. monitor the time.
5. Note that this moderator should practice their leadership skills and make sure everyone gets a chance to speak and share their opinions.
6. Next, have students begin the activity by responding with their "True or False" cards (e.g., by holding the card up so everyone can see, or placing it forward on their desks).
7. It is important that everyone shares their answers and why they chose a certain answer. Remind students that they can change their answers after they have heard what others have to say. This is a core part of the activity as it allows students to interact and share ideas while allowing the flexibility for students to change their opinions and thoughts.
8. After each student expresses their opinion and the group has time to modify their responses, if needed, the moderator will write the number of students who answered True or False. (These answers can be used during the post-activity discussion questions.)

Post-activity discussion questions:

1. How did you like this activity?
2. Were you surprised to see different responses? What surprised you most?
3. How do you feel right now? How did you feel before this activity?
4. What did you learn most from this activity?
5. What's needed to prevent bullying in school?

Key take-away message:

There are many myths and misunderstandings about bullying, so it's important to see the whole picture and how we are all involved. Understanding our beliefs about bullying is also important so we can take the next step of helping one another when we witness bullying.

Bullying is a form of aggression where someone uses their power repeatedly to purposefully abuse someone physically, emotionally or verbally. A fight between two students of equal power or those who are friends is not usually considered bullying; bullying is an unfair fight where the bully has some advantage or power over the person who is victimized.

Bullying is about power—the abuse of power. Don't let another day go by where bullies are cool and not punished for their actions. It's not okay to make people feel humiliated and abused. Life is too short, and people have enough problems. So, if you ever witness or get bullied, report it and speak up. No one deserves to be abused. Period.

(Encourage students to come to you if they want to report or talk about a problem they have.)

Material for Option 1 Activity

*The teacher reads each statement, and the class moves to the side of the room that applies.

True or False Bullying Statements

1. **Bullying usually begins in high school. FALSE**
   a. Most studies from different countries show that bullying occurs in kindergarten and that aggressive behavior can start as early as preschool. However, bullying and its effects get more severe during high school because students are more concerned with their image, being popular, feeling accepted/part of a peer group and making friends.

   Q: Have you ever noticed bullying in elementary school?

2. **Boys often bully with aggressive physical behaviors, while girls bully with words. TRUE**
   a. Boys tend to engage in more direct physical bullying, such as pushing and shoving. Girls are more prone to cyberbullying, using harsh words, gossiping or excluding a peer.

   Q: Who bullies more, boys or girls? Why do you think that is? Which type of bullying is worse, physical or verbal?

3. **Most bullying takes place when adults are around. FALSE**
   a. Bullies typically time their bullying and make sure it occurs where there is limited or no adult supervision, including at lunchtime, in the bathroom, on buses, between class periods, and at recess.
   b. Often, when adults do observe bullying behaviors, they are unsure of how to handle the situation or how to react in a helpful manner.

   Q: Have you ever witnessed bullying when an adult or supervisor was around? What did they do? How did they react?

4. **Bullies generally enjoy making others feel bad in order to make themselves feel better. TRUE**
    a. There are several reasons for bullying behavior:
        - Bullies enjoy watching a weaker child undergo humiliation.
        - Bullies like what it can do to their social status and popularity.
        - Bullies can hope to gain money or personal items from the target and feel powerful.
        - Bullies lack empathy for the target.
        - Bullies lack understanding and acceptance of the target's differences.
        - Bullies justify inflicting abuse onto others because they think their targets "deserve it."

    Q: *Have you ever bullied someone and felt superior after? Did you feel sorry for the target? Where did you learn it's okay to hurt people? Who taught you this and how can we re-wire your brain?*

Note to teacher: If you find a student who displays direct behavior of bullying and shows no acceptance and understanding of the effect(s) of his/her behavior, speak to them privately and ask them to see you after class. Discuss and educate on empathy, if possible; otherwise, plan for an intervention.

5. **Being bullied is a normal part of life and will only make you stronger. FALSE**
    a. Bullying is not a normal part of life and should not be tolerated. It is disrespectful and people need to be taught that it's not funny or to be taken lightly. We are all responsible for supporting or allowing such behavior.
    b. Bullying doesn't always make you stronger. Bullying weakens you morally and stunts your growth towards becoming a wholesome person.
    c. Bullying severely damages the reputation and self-worth of the target.
    Targets of bullying usually feel loneliness, low self-esteem, physically ill, depressed, embarrassed, afraid of coming to school and sometimes suicidal.

Q: How would you like to feel these things? It's not a joke.

6. **Most bullies are considered "cool" and people admire their toughness. TRUE**
   Q: What do you think: Are bullies in this school cool or considered popular amongst the majority? If your parents or teachers saw their "toughness" or bullying behavior, would they think it's cool?

7. **Most bystanders try to copy/imitate bullies and accept what they do because they are intimidated by the bully. TRUE**
   a. Most bystanders (people witnessing the abuse) encourage and support the bully (especially by doing nothing and not reporting the abuse).
   b. Most people are too scared to stop bullies because they don't want to get involved or be the next target.
   c. Bystanders feel powerless and anxious when they witness bullying.
   d. Most bystanders don't defend the target. They often join in, laugh, point, and smile or do nothing to intercede.
   e. Some bystanders think bullying is entertaining or funny.
   f. Bystanders often become desensitized to negative behaviors and repress feelings of empathy for bullying targets.
   g. Many bystanders think the target "deserves" such abuse or humiliation.

   Q: Do you agree? Do you think targets deserve to be abused, criticized or humiliated?

   If so, where did you learn such hatred? Where did you learn that disrespecting others is okay? Where did you learn that it's okay to hurt others? How would you like to be in their shoes?

8. **If the majority of students got together and told the bully/bullies to "STOP," bullying would still continue. FALSE**
   a. There is power in numbers. Together we can stop bullying and save lives.

b. Thousands of kids have committed suicide, some feel horrible every day because we let it happen.

Q: Are you happy knowing you are part of the problem and are the reason for students' depression?

c. Most bystanders don't like to witness bullying and know it's wrong in their hearts but feel powerless.
d. Some people think that if you ignore bullying, it will stop. This is not false. Bullying must not be ignored. It must be reported and settled as a whole, in and outside of school. But we need everyone's help to stand up and not tolerate bullying.

Q: Do you want to stop bullying or do you want to help promote it? It's your choice.

9. **Bullying behaviors in and out of school (e.g., cyber) are often reported to parents and teachers by targets and bystanders. FALSE.**
    a. Targets and bystanders often feel like authority figures cannot protect them and there is nothing they could do to help.
    b. Targets/bystanders feel that adults won't understand.
    c. Targets/bystanders feel that telling a teacher, counselor or parent will only make the situation worse.
    d. Targets/bystanders don't want to be perceived as a "tattle tale."

Q: Would you rather be a tattletale or a lifesaver?

If you were a teacher or parent, and your child was being bullied every day online and at school, what would you do? How would you feel? (Note that this is how parents feel every day.)

10. **You are ready and willing to stand up against bullying. You are ready to be leaders and help prevent bullying because you know in your heart that it's wrong and you want it to stop. TRUE**
    a. *Wonderful! Great!*
    b. Do you want bullying to stop in this school? Are you ready to stand up for your peers? Are you ready to be righteous leaders at this school and make a difference? If so, step up now.

Copy, cut, and paste the following True or False signs to each side of the classroom wall.

FALSE

TRUE

PREVENTING BULLYING:
A Manual For Teachers In Promoting Global Educational Harmony

True or False Bullying Statements

	TRUE	FALSE
1. Bullying usually begins in high school.		
2. Boys often bully with aggressive physical behaviors, while girls bully with words.		
3. Most bullying takes place when adults are around.		
4. Bullies generally enjoy making others feel bad in order to make themselves feel better.		
5. Being bullied is a normal part of life and will only make you stronger.		
6. Most bullies are considered "cool" and people admire their toughness.		
7. Most bystanders try to copy/imitate bullies and accept what they do because they are intimidated by the bully.		
8. If the majority of students got together and told the bully/bullies to "STOP," bullying would still continue.		
9. Bullying behaviors that occur in and outside of school are often reported to parents and teachers.		

Copy, cut, and distribute the following True and False boxes to each person in the class (except for moderators).

TRUE	TRUE	TRUE
TRUE	TRUE	TRUE
TRUE	TRUE	TRUE
TRUE	TRUE	TRUE
TRUE	TRUE	TRUE
TRUE	TRUE	TRUE
TRUE	TRUE	TRUE
TRUE	TRUE	TRUE
TRUE	TRUE	TRUE
TRUE	TRUE	TRUE
TRUE	TRUE	TRUE
TRUE	TRUE	TRUE

PREVENTING BULLYING:
A Manual For Teachers In Promoting Global Educational Harmony

FALSE	FALSE	FALSE
FALSE	FALSE	FALSE
FALSE	FALSE	FALSE
FALSE	FALSE	FALSE
FALSE	FALSE	FALSE
FALSE	FALSE	FALSE
FALSE	FALSE	FALSE
FALSE	FALSE	FALSE
FALSE	FALSE	FALSE
FALSE	FALSE	FALSE
FALSE	FALSE	FALSE
FALSE	FALSE	FALSE

Activity #16: "Step Up If" — Identifying Student Commonalities

<u>Activity goal:</u> To help students "step up," admit, and identify whether they have ever bullied, witnessed, or been a target of bullying.

<u>Approximate activity time:</u> 30 minutes

<u>Materials required:</u> Tape, string or any other form marking the division of the classroom

<u>Step-by-step activity process:</u>

1. Introduce the activity to students by letting them know that this exercise will give them an opportunity to "step up" and speak out about whether they have been a bully, target or bystander.
2. Clear a large open space in the room by moving all chairs and desks to one side of the room.
3. Have students stand and make a single straight line on one side of the room where they can step forward (or if there's a lot of room, cross the room).
4. Explain the activity by telling students to step forward if the statement applies to them.
5. Note that the topic is about bullying and whether they have contributed to bullying behaviors.
6. Remind students that most people are involved in bullying behaviors without even knowing it. Sometimes we can be modeling aggressive behavior learned from our parents, peers or media images and forget the effects on others. It is important that we wake up and realize that what we're doing is wrong and hurtful, and the statements provided will let us know whether we're contributing to these negative and unkind behaviors.

7. State that their honesty and participation is very important for their learning and for their peers. Being in denial won't help you understand your actions or make you grow as a person. We want to acknowledge our mistakes and try to become better people. No one is perfect, but it's important to watch our behaviors and be reminded that we may be hurting people and must stop.
8. After the activity, thank all students for their honesty and participation.

Step up Challenge:

Step up if …

1. You like being with friends.
2. You think you're generally a nice person.
3. You worry about how you look in the morning before school (like most teens).
4. You have ever been made fun of because of the way you looked or dressed. (How did it feel? What did you do?)
5. Your nationality or religion has ever been made fun of. (How did it feel? What did you do?)
6. You have ever posted an unattractive video or picture of someone on a public forum, e.g., Facebook. (This is a form of cyberbullying and is most common nowadays and extremely hurtful when so many people witness it.)
7. You have forwarded a video that might humiliate someone's reputation.
8. You have ever witnessed bullying in this school and did not report it.
9. You have ever pushed or shoved someone in public.
10. You have known/know someone who has thought about committing suicide.
11. You have ever ignored or excluded someone in school. (Why? How did you feel after?)
12. You have ever been excluded. (How did it feel? What did you do?)
13. You gave someone "cut-eyes/angry eyes" or "elevator eyes," looking them up and down. (This is a form of non-verbal abuse.)
14. You think you're cooler than most people in school.
15. You have ever confronted a bully and told them to stop. (Note that this is difficult so you can report it and get help.)
16. You have befriended a target of bullying because you understood their pain.
17. You are going to be more compassionate and step up if you see someone bullied, because you understand what it feels like, and know it's wrong.

PREVENTING BULLYING:
A Manual For Teachers In Promoting Global Educational Harmony

Post-activity discussion questions:

1. After hearing these statements, do you think you could be a bully?
2. What did you learn from this activity?
3. What did you learn about yourself?
4. Where do you learn to be disrespectful to one another?
5. Have you ever been peer pressured to do something you knew was wrong?
6. What do you think is your worst behavior?
7. What can you do to make things better with the person you hurt?
8. How can you avoid doing or saying these things in the future?
9. Do you think most people are bad and bullies? (Reply: All people are inherently good. No one is pure evil. Wait, be patient, and give them the opportunity to show themselves; get to know them and hear their stories of why they act this way.)

Key take-away message:

You are not alone in your suffering and negative behaviors. Sometimes we hurt people subconsciously because of peer pressure or simply because we've been taught it's okay or cool to insult or abuse our power over others, making us feel superior. Students are left feeling depressed, rejected by their peers, ridiculed, attacked or insulted online, and understandably, end up contemplating suicide. So, we are all responsible for each other's suffering and we should be acutely aware of our actions and words.

Stepping up takes bravery and strength. Apologize to those you hurt and then forgive yourself and vow never to do harm again because your negative actions will also haunt you and you cannot take back the words, insults or threats that you made. No one is perfect and we must grow and continuously become better and kinder people.

(Encourage students to come to you if they want to report or talk about a problem they have.)

Activity #17: Write Your Truth About Bullying and Post It Anonymously

Activity goal: To have students express their honest feelings about bullying and what they witness or experience on anonymous cards that everyone can learn from. Teachers will then collect the cards and post them publicly on display for everyone in the class or the school to read.

Approximate activity time: 20 minutes

Materials required: Printouts of "Share Your Truth" papers, pens/pencils (same color and type to help with anonymity)

Step-by-step activity process:

1. Have students sit in an area of the room that is private.
2. Explain the task of expressing your feelings anonymously about bullying in and out of school.
3. Copy, cut and distribute the "Share Your Truth" papers.
4. Read and explain the cards.

Here is an example:

"SHARE YOUR TRUTH" STUDENT EXAMPLES
(For Teachers' Use)

I think bullying is ... *(Students' opinion) E.g., wrong, foolish, about power and control, mostly done online, popular among girls, hurtful, funny, done to copy others or be popular.*

I've ... *(Students' experience or witnessing of bullying) E.g., experienced bullying every day in elementary school, online from people I thought were friends, in the halls by having people call me a slut, laughing at the way I dress, making fun of my sexuality, nationality, religion or skin color)*

Final thoughts: ... *(Ways to stop bullying) E.g., I think we should have a bully-free day, a time when people listen to each other's stories and experiences. I think we should learn to be friends and accept each other's differences.*

---

5. Next play some soft music while they write their ideas, experiences or feelings about bullying.
6. Ask students to all use the same color pen or pencil to make it completely anonymous.
7. Tell students to be as open and honest as possible to express themselves and to help others learn about bullying and how they are not alone in their fears or experiences.
8. Tell students to look at their own papers and that this exercise is confidential.
9. After about 5–10 minutes, check to see if everyone has completed their cards.
10. Optional: Ask the class if they would like to share their responses.
11. Thank students for their honesty and participation.
12. Collect the paper. Post the papers on a poster or pin board for everyone to see on display, titled "Students' Truth About Bullying."

Post-activity discussion questions:

1. How was this exercise? Difficult or easy?
2. What was the easiest question? What was the most difficult?
3. Do you think students will read these?
4. How will students feel when they read your response?
5. What are some other things we can do together as a class to help stop bullying in and out of school?

Key take-away message:

Everyone has a story. No one's life is perfect. The bullies have a story and reason for their actions and so do the bystanders. But the targets are the ones who are suffering and contemplating their life and self-worth. Why should they do this?

You all have a voice. It's important to speak up and tell people about how you feel, what you witness or if you ever get bullied. No one should endure pain or humiliation or any kind of abuse. You must tell someone if you are ever feeling down or being abused. People are there to help you. A first step is having a support group that understands what you are going through. So, open yourself up to others. Trust one another. Help one another. And imagine it was you or your sibling getting hurt. We must have compassion and realize the pain many students are going through. I hope your words will console others who also feel lost, hurt or confused about bullying.

"Share Your Truth" Student Papers

SHARE YOUR TRUTH

Bullying is …

I've …

Final thoughts:

SHARE YOUR TRUTH

Bullying is …

I've …

Final thoughts:

Step 4: Cultivate Moments of Empathy and Morality

In order to change students' behaviors and the way they feel about bullying, it is essential to utilize an experiential learning approach, encompassing exercises and activities that engage students to think about power, experience true empathy, and feel empowered to help stop bullying. At this stage, it is most important for students (bullies in particular) to learn *first-hand how* it feels to be on the receiving end of bullying (done sensitively and systematically), so they are motivated to not do unto others as they would not want to be done to themselves.

> *"A major and inescapable goal of educational institutions is to broaden the perspectives of human beings, to develop a truly functional empathy, to free human beings from the constrictions of ignorance, superstition, hostility, and other forms of inhumanity."*
>
> — Kenneth Clark, Noted Child Psychologist

Activity #18: Walk in Their Shoes; An Experiential Learning Exercise

<u>Activity goal:</u> Students will answer a series of questions related to different bullying scenarios (e.g., verbal, cyber, physical and non-verbal) and explore how it feels to be either a bully, target, bystander or helper.

*Note that this activity is very influential and must be done with caution and care.

<u>Approximate activity time:</u> 30 minutes

<u>Materials required:</u> paper/notebook, pens/pencils, bullying roles (*provided below*), and bullying scenarios printouts (*for teacher's use only*)

<u>Step-by-step activity process:</u>

1. Paste the "Group Roles" labels (i.e., bullies, bystanders, targets and helpers) provided below in four separate areas of the classroom.
2. Introduce the activity by telling students that this exercise will give them an opportunity to experience what it feels like for everyone involved in a bullying situation.
3. Copy, cut and have students randomly select their roles from a hat, or randomly assign student roles making sure students are NOT placed with close friends in the same group.
4. Make sure there is an even number for each group, helping students not feel so "alone" in their roles.
5. Have students get into groups according to their role and sit in the four corners of the room facing each other.
    a. Targets
    b. Bystanders
    c. Bullies
    d. Helpers

*Remind students that this is an exercise where they can imagine how it feels to be in this position, which will enable us all to be more conscious of our words and actions.

6. Make sure each student has paper or a notebook and pencil to take notes on and write their feelings during this exercise.
7. Review each of the group's roles so students become familiar with them. (Optional: put a collar or label on the Targets, Bullies and Bystanders so the class can identify them from afar and they get a deeper sense of how it feels to be in these roles. Automatically with the label on, emotions will begin to shift, and students will begin to associate with their given roles.)

***What is important is for the teacher NOT to assign common targets of bullying as the targets since they already have endured enough suffering in their everyday lives. It is recommended to put them in the bystander or helper group.

8. Next, ask each group to imagine themselves in these roles and to take their position seriously for the length of time given for this exercise.

    The goal of the exercise is for students to understand what they do to each other including: verbal, physical, emotional/non-verbal and cyber/online abuse.

9. Begin the activity by reading each scenario (provided below), allowing students to recall all the types of bullying that commonly occur.
10. After reading the scenarios, ask each group member to write the following:
    a. three words to describe how they are feeling in this role.
    b. how they perceive the others in opposite groups.
    c. three ways they can help respond to bullying in their roles.
11. After 3–5 minutes of allowing them to write, ask each group to share their thoughts and talk directly to each group.
12. After the exercise, thank students for their honesty and participation.
13. Then, tell students to sit in a large circle, remove their labels and process the activity.

PREVENTING BULLYING:
A Manual For Teachers In Promoting Global Educational Harmony

<u>Post-activity discussion questions:</u>

1. How did it feel to be labeled?
2. What role is the most difficult?
3. What role is the easiest?
4. What did you learn from this exercise?
5. What is the most common reason why bystanders do not help or stand up for targets?
6. What would happen if they did? What are some ways they can?
7. What could they say to them?
8. Can one person actually make a difference?

<u>Key take-away message:</u>

Role-playing helps put us in someone else's shoes and teaches us to empathize with that person. Playing out these roles of receiver, giver and friend allows us to think about how we would act in such roles and question what else we could be doing.

Bullying Scenarios
For Teachers & Facilitation Use Only

Scenario 1: Verbal Abuse

_____ (a target) is walking the halls and some girls say, "Look at what she's wearing, she's such a loser."

_____ (a target) is in gym class and _____ (a bully's name) calls him a "fag" and to stay away from him.

_____ (bullies) calls you (a target): metal mouth, slut, faggot, smelly, stupid, nerds, Pinocchio or a terrorist … every day.

S1 Questions:

A. What are 3 words to describe how you are feeling right now?
B. How do you think the (a) bullies, (b) targets, (c) bystanders feel?
C. How does your group perceive the other students (in their given roles)?
D. What can the target do right now? How should they respond?
E. What are some ways to manage this stress?
F. What are some ways the bystanders can help? What can the target do if no one helps?

Go deeper:

What gives bullies the right to say these things? Don't you think it's humiliating and disrespectful? Why does everyone have to be, look and dress like you to be accepted? Where did they learn it was okay? Where and how did bystanders become so afraid? Where is your compassion for others? Where can you learn compassion and respect? Why has being rude become popular or funny? Do bullies feel more powerful when they say these things? Have you bullies ever gotten verbally abused? If so, by whom and how did it feel?

PREVENTING BULLYING:
A Manual For Teachers In Promoting Global Educational Harmony

Scenario 2: Physical Abuse

_____ (a target) was walking in the halls when _____ (a bully's name) tripped him/her and started laughing in his face.

_____ (a target) walked out of school towards the bus stop and _____ (a bully's name) pushed him and said, "What are you looking at?"

_____ (a target) would sit in class and have people shoot pens, erasers or papers at them.

S2 Questions:

A. What are 3 words to describe how you are feeling right now?
B. How do you think the (a) bullies, (b) targets, (c) bystanders feel?
C. How does your group perceive the other students (in their given roles)?
D. What can the target do right now? How should they respond?
E. What are some ways the bystanders can help? What can the target do if no one helps?

Go deeper:

How would you feel if I pushed you every day, cornered you or shoved you in the locker? Stand up if you've ever been pushed. Did you want someone to do it again? Did you fight back? What will fighting back do? What is the purpose of physical aggression? Who wins? Who feels powerful and powerless? Physical aggressiveness is about the power that people seek, and bystanders think it's entertaining. Do you like watching people suffer? Do you think society has become numb and desensitized to people's hurt? Are you proud of this? Are you proud of knowing so many students at our school are being abused verbally and physically?

Scenario 3: Non-verbal

_____ (a target) walked into class and everyone started laughing and whispering about her.

_____ (a target) walked to the cafeteria and all her friends just ignored her and looked away because of something that happened at a party.

_____ (a target) walked on the bus while everyone avoided him and blocked their seats with their bags.

_____ (a bully) gave _____ (a target) "angry eyes" or rolled them each time they spoke or when walking in the halls.

_____ (a bully) turned all his/her friends against____(a target).

They had no one to sit with at lunch or talk to every day about their pain or joys. Old friends would prank call them at night, then look away and ignore them each time they were near each other. How could you do this to your friends? What is a real friend anyway? Does a real friend kick you when you're down, or help you get back up in times of need? How can you watch people suffer and feel lonely, then carry on with your day? Imagine it was you. Do you feel more powerful watching others in pain?

S3 Questions:

  A. What are 3 words to describe how you are feeling right now?
  B. How do you think the (a) bully, (b) target, and (c) bystanders feel?
  C. How does your group perceive the other students (in their given roles)?
  D. What can the target do right now? How should they respond?
  E. What are some ways the bystanders can help? What can the target do if no one helps?

Go deeper:

How would you like to be rejected and ridiculed by everyone? Would you like to try it? I would like everyone to turn away and look away from the bystanders. Don't talk to them. Don't look at them. Roll your eyes at them. Walk away from them if you see them approaching you.

- How do you bystanders feel? Will anyone help you? Did you help others when they were alone? Now it's your turn. Who will pick you up when you fall?

Next, have the targets place their labels or collars (pieces of materials around their necks) and place it around the people in the bystander group. Change the large group labels.

*Note that all these roles are temporary and part of the exercise, but in reality, this is how so many students feel on a daily basis and they can just slip out of these roles because no one is letting or helping them.

Scenario 4: Cyberbullying

Cut, copy and distribute the cyberbullying example to each student (see below).

Focus on the new "targets." Ask them to read the email or text message they just received.

S4 Questions:

A. What are 3 words to describe how you are feeling right now?
B. How do you think the (a) bullies, (b) targets, (c) bystanders feel?
C. How does your group perceive the other students (in their given roles)?
D. What can the target do right now? How should they respond? What can the target do if no one helps?
E. What are some ways the bystanders can help?

*** Refer to: "How to Respond to Cyberbullying"

Go deeper:

How does your body feel when reading this? Does it feel real? This is real for millions of students. How would you feel if you received this? What would you do? How would you like it if the whole school saw what was sent to you or if the whole school wrote these things about you on a public forum? Would you want to come to school the next day?

(Pause.)

Have you ever written something similar to this? Do you know anyone who has written something like this? Are you proud of it or being part of it? Do you feel good about making people sick to their stomachs? Do you not have empathy for others? If you did, you would have stopped it. What can you do in the future to stop this?

PREVENTING BULLYING:
A Manual For Teachers In Promoting Global Educational Harmony

Cut and distribute a copy to each student.

> Go back to your country.
>
> No one likes you.
>
> You should kill yourself.
>
> You're retarded.
>
> We're gonna get you after school.
>
> Send me a sex pic or I'll tell everyone what you did.

Christina Theophilos, M.Ed. & Raju Ramanathan, M.Tech

Bullying Roles & Labels
Cut, copy and distribute to each student.

BULLY
TARGET
BYSTANDER
HELPERS

Activity #19: Explore Bullying Roles — Small Group Discussion

<u>Activity goal:</u> To continue with role-playing different situations while answering a series of questions. This activity is exceptionally powerful and effective because it gives each "bullying role" a voice and a chance to be heard and is expressed by peers.

<u>Approximate activity time:</u> 60 minutes

<u>Materials required:</u> Role assignment labels, role play questions (*provided below*)

<u>Step-by-step activity process:</u>

1. Introduce the activity to students by explaining to them that they will be role-playing being a bully, target or bystander to experience what it feels like to be in each role.
2. Randomly divide the class into 4 groups: (1) bullies, (2) targets, (3) bystanders and (4) helpers
   (*Consisting of a mix of introverts and extroverts. Avoid having friends in the same group). See tips for teachers on *Making Random Groups.*
3. Copy, cut and distribute each group label where they are seated. Ask each group to sit in a tightly closed circle. Copy, cut and distribute the questions about bullies, targets, bystanders and helpers to each selected group.
4. Have each group answer the questions about either bullies, targets or bystanders (10–15 minutes)
5. Once they are done, have each group stand and present their answers.
6. Thank everyone and ask them to remove their labels and return to their seats.

Post-activity discussion questions:

1. How did you feel in your roles?
2. Did it feel realistic?
3. What did you learn from this activity?
4. What will you remember most?
5. What did you learn about yourself from this activity?
6. What role or group do you belong to?

Key take-away message:

It's important to know what it feels like to be a bully, target, helper and bystander so one can better understand them and be brave enough to step up and stop bullying when one witnesses or experiences it. Targets should seek help and not feel ashamed to do so. There are always people there to help. Showing empathy for a target's situation shows that we care, and that is important for everyone. Treat others as you want to be treated. A bystander is part of the problem and they must help targets because one day, it can be themselves (karma). Everyone wants to be a helper, but they don't always have the strength or courage. Bullying is preventable if everyone works together to understand each other, communicate and act kindly towards one another.

PREVENTING BULLYING:
A Manual For Teachers In Promoting Global Educational Harmony

Role-Play Questions

Copy, cut and distribute.

GROUP 1: BULLIES

1. What is a bully?
2. What are some common characteristics of a bully? What do they usually look like?
3. Who do they usually bully?
4. What are some common examples of bullying in and outside
5. of school?
6. What are some reasons why people bully?
7. Where do they learn this behavior?

Roleplay as Bullies

1. Describe words to express how you feel as a bully?
2. How do you think people perceive you?
3. How do you perceive targets, bystanders and helpers?

GROUP 2: TARGETS

1. What are some examples of being a target of bullying at school?
2. What are some common characteristics of a target of bullying?
3. If the usual target isn't around, who will they bully next?
4. What happens physically, socially, emotionally and academically when someone is bullied?
5. What can targets do or say to stop the bullying from happening again?
6. Do you know any targets of bullying in this school? Did you ever help them or report that they are being bullied? Why or why not?

Roleplay as Targets

1. Describe words to express how you feel as targets of bullying?
2. How do you think people perceive you?
3. How do you perceive bullies, bystanders and helpers?

GROUP 3: BYSTANDERS

1. What are bystanders?
2. What are some common characteristics of a bystander?
3. How do they influence bullying from happening?
4. Why don't bystanders help targets of bullying?
5. Have you ever witnessed bullying?
6. What did you do?
7. What could bystanders do to help targets of bullying?

Roleplay as Bystanders

1. Describe words to express how you feel as bystanders?
2. How do you think people perceive you?
3. How do you perceive targets, bullies and helpers?

GROUP 4: HELPERS

1. What can helpers do to support a target of bullying?
2. What are some characteristics of someone who is a helper/defender of bullying?
3. On average, what percentage of students in this school help stop bullying?
4. How are helpers perceived by others?
5. Would you like to date someone who is a bully or a helper?
6. If you were a helper, how would you feel?

Roleplay as Targets

1. Describe words to express how you feel as helpers/defenders of bullying?
2. How do you think people perceive you?
3. How do you perceive targets, bystanders and bullies?

PREVENTING BULLYING:
A Manual For Teachers In Promoting Global Educational Harmony

Group Labels 1

Copy, cut and distribute.

1. Bullies

2. Targets

3. Bystanders

4. Helpers

Group Labels 2

Copy, cut and distribute.

1) Bully	1) Bully	1) Bully
2) Target	2) Target	2) Target
3) Bystander	3) Bystander	3) Bystander
4) Helper	4) Helper	4) Helper
1) Bully	1) Bully	1) Bully
2) Target	2) Target	2) Target
3) Bystander	3) Bystander	3) Bystander
4) Helper	4) Helper	4) Helper
1) Bully	1) Bully	1) Bully
2) Target	2) Target	2) Target
3) Bystander	3) Bystander	3) Bystander
4) Helper	4) Helper	4) Helper

Activity #20: The Use and Abuse of Power — Round Circle Discussion

<u>Activity goal:</u> For students to reflect upon the use of power and control over others to make themselves feel superior. Students will sit in a circle and share stories of when they felt most powerful and then discuss the power dynamic in school and in society, and its effects on others.

<u>Approximate activity time:</u> 30–45 minutes

<u>Materials required:</u> None

<u>Step-by-step activity process:</u>

1. Inform students of the topic of discussion in this activity: The use of power in school and society and its effect on others, which leads to bullying behaviors.
2. Ask students to sit on the floor or on chairs in a closed circle. (Going outside in nature is also optional.)
3. Ask students:
   a. What makes someone powerful in our society?
   b. What are some examples of powerful people in society?
   c. What common characteristics do they have? (E.g., strength, money, status, position, contacts, material things, inspiration, leadership, gender, religion, sexual orientation, nationality, skin color, appearance, skills, intelligence)
   d. What makes someone powerful in groups? (E.g., attitude, age, speech, character, voice, posture, social status, intelligence, height, skills and material things like the coolest shoes, car, or house)
   e. Is a bully powerful? How does a bully become powerful? Do you admire bullies or see what they do as entertaining?
   f. How do bullies convince the group majority to fear and follow them? What skills do they have?
   g. How do bullies abuse their power? What effects does it have on others?

h. Where do we learn about power? (E.g., parents, siblings, media, peers, teachers)
4. Next, ask students to think of a time they felt most powerful (e.g., with friends, family, school, sports). Either go around in a circle or randomly select the next person so they don't wait for their turn with fear.
5. Ask students to practice listening with an open heart, not interrupt or judge.
6. Begin sharing "experiences of power." (The teacher can lead by example and share their story.)
   a. *"I've felt powerful when..."*

Post-activity discussion questions:

1. How much power do you have in your circle of friends or at school?
2. Do you use your power to help others or yourself?
3. Do you mainly use your power to do good or bad on others?
4. How do bullies use their power to control others? (E.g., threats, dominance, insults)
5. How do you think bullies feel when they abuse others verbally, physically or online?
6. How do you think the target feels? Why do we respect bullies so much and let them get away with what they do?
7. Do you think our views about power and control in society or in school are just?
8. How can you use your power to help others? How much power do you have? (Encourage students that they have a lot of power and the right to a safe learning environment and life. They are not alone, and people are there to help.)
9. Who do you think is the most powerful or influential in this class and why?
10. Do you think there is power in numbers? What if everyone in this circle told the bully to stop their behavior and report it to authorities, would that be powerful?

PREVENTING BULLYING:
A Manual For Teachers In Promoting Global Educational Harmony

Key take-away message:

Bullying is essentially the abuse of power. It involves psychologically, verbally or physically making the target feel inferior. Anyone can be bullied or harassed in their lifetime. It is usually learned at home, whereupon it is transferred to or experienced in school. We learn about the abuse of power perhaps from our parents and how they treat others, or from the media, and then copy this learned behavior at school, where it translates into bullying. People who usually bully others seek control or authority that they don't have in other areas in their life.

Therefore, it's important that we stop admiring aggressive, powerful bullies and seek help or report it right away if we ever witness or experience someone abusing their power. Not seeking help means allowing the bullying to continue, affecting any of us someday. So, one must learn how to stand up for oneself and others. We must protect one another and respect each other. There is power in numbers, and even alone, we can use our power to do good.

Activity #21: Understand the Effects of Bullying

<u>Activity goal:</u> To build empathy among students for targets of bullying and to familiarize students with some of the consequences of harassment in and outside of school.

<u>Approximate activity time:</u> 30–45 minutes

<u>Materials required:</u> Bullying Type Worksheets (*provided below*)

<u>Step-by-step activity process:</u>

1. Explain the topic of the activity to students, i.e., understanding the consequences of being a *target* and a bully.
2. Encourage openness, sharing and listening to everyone's perspective.
3. Ask students:
    a. What are some common examples of bullying that you've witnessed or experienced either: (a) verbal, (b) physical, (c) emotional or (d) online?
    b. What are some possible consequences for the target? (E.g., anxiety, thoughts of suicide, embarrassment, loss of concentration in school, low self-esteem, loss of friends)
    c. How do you feel knowing so many people are feeling this way, perhaps in our school or classroom? How would you feel if you were in their shoes?
    d. How do you feel when you see someone being bullied? (E.g., it's not your problem, scared, sad)
    e. How might you feel if you are the bully?
    f. How has bullying become so popular? How did society become so insensitive, numb and lack empathy? Where did we learn this? (E.g., the media, violence, power, parents, siblings)
4. Next, divide the class into 4 groups and have them sit in a close circle or square where all members feel included.
5. Copy, cut and distribute the worksheets to each group.

6. Review group task:
    a. Students will brainstorm and write examples of the type of bullying assigned to their group: (1) verbal, (2) physical, (3) emotional (non-verbal), (4) online.
        i. Each group is asked similar questions on:
        ii. Examples (realistic scenarios) of the type of bullying given to their group.
        iii. How the target may possibly feel in this situation and effects on the person's body, mind or behavior.
        iv. How the bystanders feel witnessing this abuse.
        v. How the bully feels and the outcomes (e.g., consequences/punishments) for the bully.
7. Tell students they will have 15 minutes to complete their answers as a team and then ask to have 1 or 2 speakers from each group stand up and present their group's bullying type and answers.
8. Again, encourage openness, sharing, listening to everyone's perspective and understanding of others' feelings. Note that this is a serious issue, and we must learn to empathize with others and what students are experiencing daily. Maybe some students are doing these forms of bullying and forget the impact they have on others. Hopefully, through this exercise, we will see that bullying is not "just a joke." It's serious, causing depression and suicidal thoughts every day. Everyone needs to work together to first understand the impact on targets and then find solutions for bullying prevention.
9. Ask the students to begin and to complete the exercise seriously and with an open heart.
10. Give students about 15 minutes to complete the exercise. Walk around the class to see if they have any questions and check their completion time.
11. After they have completed their question sheets, ask each group to assign a spokesperson(s) to present their answers.
12. Thank each group for their efforts and honesty.

Post-activity discussion questions:

1. Can we really understand what bullying feels like? (Let's close our eyes for a moment and imagine this happened to you. That you felt alone hurt and scared. This isn't a joke. We are all part of the problem and can all be part of the solution. You must walk in their shoes, and we all know what pain feels like so we must not let it happen to others. This is the only logical and humanitarian thing to do. Help each other at all costs.)
2. Now, which form of bullying do you think is the worst? (Answer: All forms are terrible, humiliating and hurtful, but online bullying seems to be worse and most common since the harasser may hide their identity and face, making it easier to say things they would not do or say publicly.)
3. What can happen to a person's identity and self-esteem if they are bullied every day? (Answer: They may lose their self-concept, confidence and overall positive outlook on life.)
4. What do you think happens: (a) physically, (b) emotionally, (c) intellectually, and (d) socially? See Bullying Outcomes.
5. How would your life change if you were a target? Is it possible for you to become a target one day? Why or why not? (Note that in high school, many students tend to reject their friends because of something they did or said. Not having friends is a terrible feeling. So, it's up to you to include everyone and make them feel good. Life is too short not to try. Be real leaders and students that care for one another, despite your differences.)
6. How would you feel walking in the halls alone? (Note that: everyone wants to be loved and accepted and we should try to make everyone feel that way.)
7. Knowing about all these terrible outcomes, will you continue to bully or watch others be targets of bullying? Will you report bullying next time you experience or witness it?
   What happens at this school if a bullying incident is reported? (See "Effective Ways of Dealing with Bullying: Sanctions and Consequences" section and share this information on how

8. What do you think is the most effective consequence that can be given to bullies? Why?
9. Do you think harsh consequences can help prevent bullying? (What about getting the police involved and having a criminal record? Would this be effective?)
10. If you knew that bullies tend to become abusers as adults with their spouse or children (since they crave control and authority using abuse or aggression), would you still think they were cool?
11. How has being aggressive and abusive come to equal power and high social status? Do you think the abusive people in school are powerful and cool? If not, why do you encourage them?
12. What can happen to a target of bullying in a positive way?
13. What might he/she learn about people or life?

(Note that in the next class, you will learn how to discourage bullying.)

Key take-away message:

Bullying outcomes are extremely serious. Imagine being pushed around every day. Hearing people laugh at you and verbally insult you, including your so-called "friends," is difficult. Imagine that this bullying continues outside of school as well—on the school bus, on the internet, at home (by parents or siblings). Being a target of bullying can lead to extremely low self-esteem. Targets often experience anxiety, loneliness, low academic performance, absenteeism, family problems, and even think about committing suicide.

(Encourage students to come to you if they want to report or talk about a problem they have.)

Bullying Types Worksheet

Bullying Type 1: Verbal Abuse

What are some examples of verbal abuse in or outside of school?

What are some possible feelings and effects on the target?

What effects might this have on the bystander(s)?

What are the effects and consequences on the bully?

PREVENTING BULLYING:
A Manual For Teachers In Promoting Global Educational Harmony

Bullying Type 2: Physical Abuse

What are some examples of physical abuse in or outside of school?

What are some possible feelings and effects on the target?

What effects might this have on the bystander(s)?

What are the effects and consequences on the bully?

Bullying Type 3: Non-verbal Abuse (E.g., rolling eyes, exclusion, intimidation)

What are some examples of non-verbal abuse in or outside of school?

What are some possible feelings and effects on the target?

What effects might this have on the bystander(s)?

What are the effects and consequences on the bully?

PREVENTING BULLYING:
A Manual For Teachers In Promoting Global Educational Harmony

Bullying Type 4: Online (cyberbullying, text messages)

What are some examples of cyberbullying in or outside of school?

What are some possible feelings and effects on the target?

What effects might this have on the bystander(s)?

What are the effects and consequences on the bully?

FOUR BASIC TYPES OF BULLYING

Verbal bullying:

- Name-calling (sometimes seen as teasing)
- Harassing them to do or say something
- Spreading gossip or lies (rumors)
- Insulting one's family, status or religion
- Yelling at someone
- Insulting or nagging
- Making verbal threats or demands
- Making noise as they pass by (e.g., whistling or shouting "fag")
- Racist jokes

Physical bullying:

- Making threatening poses (fists, cornering someone)
- Sexual harassment: pinching, groping, touching
- Stealing (jacking) their lunch, money, clothing, homework or books
- Pushing, punching, pulling hair, flicking or bumping into them on purpose
- Use or showing of weapons (knife, bat or gun)
- Throwing or hiding their belongings
- Damaging their things
- Spitting, flicking paper, rubber bands or any other object
- Burping in their face

Non-verbal bullying:

- Intentional exclusion from games, sports, conversations, planned activities/parties
- Discrimination and exclusion due to the color of their skin color, religion, sexual orientation, disability
- Ignoring the person because they're not considered cool.

- Giving the "silent treatment" or "bad girl/boy attitude"
- Whispering and pointing while looking at the target
- Giving angry eyes/cut-eyes
- Sexual looks
- Sticking their tongue out
- Peer pressure to smoke, drink or steal
- Intimidating or threatening using gestures

Cyber/Online bullying:

- Voting the fattest, ugliest, least popular or worst-dressed person in the class online
- Making insulting or sarcastic comments on Facebook or other networks
- Tagging humiliating videos or pictures or sending them to other people by phone or email
- Sending abusive/nasty/threatening messages in a chat room, instant messenger or text message
- Taking someone's password or identity online and reading their messages (gossiping/invasion of privacy)
- Prank calling

Bullying Type	Bullying Outcomes
Physical	- Caused by others: bruises, scratches, cuts or ripped/stretched-out shirts - Caused by stress: headaches, backaches, stomach aches, bedwetting, loss of hair, skin disorders, sleep difficulties, nightmares, irregular menstruation, loss of appetite or overeating, pale skin, tension and weak immune system resulting in illnesses. - Caused by self: smoking, drinking, drug abuse, absenteeism, changing schools, dropping out of high school, cutting andeven suicide

Bullying Type	Bullying Outcomes
Intellectual	• Academic impact includes reduced concentration, memory difficulties in and outside of class and incomplete homework, tests, or assignments. They do not contribute or ask questions during class to avoid attention. This often results in low academic performance, high school dropouts and discontinuation of further education. • Gifted or intelligent students hide their potential and knowledge for fear of being ridiculed, thus restricting their achievements and talents. • Academically challenged students cover their disabilities or difficulties, fearing being called "stupid" or outcasts. • Suicidal thoughts
Social	• <u>Peers:</u> They avoid and feel uncomfortable around tense, insecure students (who perhaps remind them of their vulnerability). • <u>Friends:</u> They distance themselves from the target and merge with new friends, fearing being associated with the target or getting bullied themselves. Targets may be attached to one friend to feel secure and not alone. Also, they may stay in a "trendy or secure" group of friends where they are bullied yet choose to stay to feel a sense of belonging to that group. • <u>Family:</u> Parents feel helpless and inexperienced on how to help support their child. The child may isolate themselves from family members to avoid burdening or disappointing their parents.

PREVENTING BULLYING:
A Manual For Teachers In Promoting Global Educational Harmony

Bullying Type	Bullying Outcomes
	• <u>Gatherings:</u> Targets may avoid areas where they can be targeted (large crowds, school buses, cafeteria) where supervision is less noticed. As a result of their exclusion and disassociation, they are often not invited to parties, are last to join games or group projects and have a poor social life. • <u>Social skills:</u> Targets become isolated and fear being hurt and rejected again, so they often have difficulty making new friends and forget how to trust others.
Emotional	• <u>Shock:</u> Targets are usually shocked and surprised and first but then fear freezes them to do anything about it, while "disaster movies" of the worst-case scenarios and future encounters replay themselves in their heads. • <u>Sickening fear:</u> They feel like their world is unsafe from people superior to them. • <u>Learned helplessness:</u> The belief that there's nothing they can do to escape or help their situation. • <u>Depressed and angry:</u> They direct such emotions towards people they feel comfortable with, like their parents, and fantasize about revenge. • <u>Identity crisis:</u> Targets forget who they are and their self-worth and begin self-loathing or believing what the bully thinks. They feel undesirable and incapable. • <u>Hitting Rock Bottom:</u> They can't bear the distress, so they usually find solutions or seek help from others.

Activity #22: Share Feelings — "I feel… when…"

Activity goal: To encourage students to openly share experiences based on certain words presented in the activity. The emotions discussed will be a link to bullying in hopes of showing students that they are not alone in their suffering.

Approximate activity time: 30–45 minutes

Materials required: "Feeling Words" printouts, tape

Step-by-step activity process:

1. Describe the session agenda: to share feelings students have about bullying and learn about other people's perspectives.
2. Ask students to sit on the floor or on chairs in a closed circle.
3. Spread out and tape the "feeling words" to the ground in the middle of the circle.
4. Next, allow students to think about a time they have:
    a. witnessed bullying.
    b. experienced bullying.
    c. bullied others.
5. Next, have students take turns and stand on the word that best describes their feelings during a time in their life when they've witnessed, experienced or bullied others.
6. Encourage students to listen attentively with an open heart and be as honest as possible so all can learn from each other.
7. Have students begin by completing the following phrase:
   "*I feel* _____ *when* _____."
   Examples: "I feel **angry** when I witness bullying but don't know how to help."
   - "I feel **humiliated** when people insult my brother because he's disabled."
   - "I feel **confident** when I play the piano or make my friends laugh."

PREVENTING BULLYING:
A Manual For Teachers In Promoting Global Educational Harmony

- "I feel **afraid** when I go to English class because I know Joey always makes fun of me or will say something completely rude and will ruin my whole day."
- "I feel **powerful** when I make others laugh or put them down."

8. Thank everyone for their openness and honesty.

Post-activity discussion questions:

1. What do you think the purpose of this activity was?
2. What did you learn *most* from this session?
3. What was most *surprising* to you?
4. What did you *learn about yourself* from this activity?
5. What word was most *difficult* for you to express?
6. How did you *feel during* the activity?
7. How do you *feel now* that this activity is over?
8. What did we all have in common?
9. What is one thing we all want? (E.g., love, acceptance)
10. What will you *remember* most from this session?

Key take-away message:

Everyone has feelings about bullying. Most people have experienced some form of bullying as both the target and the harasser. But what we forget when we live day-to-day is that we hurt people in the way we act towards each other. No one wants to feel pain or humiliation. We know this. This is natural. Our deepest desire as humans is to connect and receive love from one another, so it's ironic that we tend to do otherwise so we can fit in with the crowd. Showing compassion to others in the way you speak or even look at them is so important. So, watch the way you act. Smile and show love to each other. Just try and you will see a world of difference in yourself and those around you.

Feeling Words

Cut, copy and paste on the floor.

AFRAID

ANGRY

HUMILIATED

POWERFUL

PROUD

COOL / POPULAR

HURT

Activity #23: Identify Students' Values — Discussion and Worksheet

<u>Activity goal:</u> To have students understand their values and how these values influence their behaviors toward accepting and respecting others. This activity hopes to instill positive values and actions.

<u>Approximate activity time:</u> 30 minutes

<u>Materials required:</u> Notebooks, pens/pencils

<u>Step-by-step activity process:</u>

1. Tell students that in this session, you will be exploring values that each of us has that might influence our behaviors toward accepting and respecting others.
2. Ask students:
   "What does it mean to value something?" (E.g., something we appreciate, follow, respect, admire; values bring us *pleasure* and *happiness*)
3. Ask students:
   "What are some examples of society's values?" (E.g., family, money, fashion, health, being active, food, popularity, power, education, friends, working hard, honesty, love, originality, nature, art, music, helping people)
4. Tell students you want them to think about what they value most, since it affects their everyday mood, attitude, future, relationships and behavior towards themselves and others.
5. Make random groups of 3–4 students and have each group sit in a tight circle, preferably not groups of friends.
6. Write the *"Understanding Your Actions and Values"* questions on the board. Have students copy and complete the questions in their notebooks.

~ OR ~

Copy, cut and distribute the *"Understanding Your Actions and Values"* sheet.

1. Leave 5–10 minutes for students to write notes and answer the questions individually. Tell students they will be asked to share their answers in small groups and to be as honest as possible.
2. After they have finished, tell students to discuss their responses and listen carefully to their groups' answers.

Post-activity discussion questions:

1. What were the common values of each group? Did you have anything in common?
2. Where do we learn our values? (E.g., parents, media, biologically, spiritually, friends)
3. What did you learn about yourself? Do you think your values make you a kind of selfish person?
4. How do your values relate to bullying in and out of school?
5. How much do you respect others or tolerate bullying? How do you demonstrate kindness and respect in school and towards your peers?

Key take-away message:

Our values reflect our actions and behavior. Therefore, it's important to understand our values, which are the driving forces of our behaviors. Sometimes our values should be shifted to more positive ones that will help our overall well-being and future. If you value kindness and respect, you should never tolerate bullying. The most important value is the COURAGE to do the right thing. Support a target, report it and stand up to the bully.

Encourage students to come to you if they want to report or talk about a problem they have.

PREVENTING BULLYING:
A Manual For Teachers In Promoting Global Educational Harmony

Understanding Your Actions and Values

(Student Worksheet)

Student Name _____

    a.   What are your top 5 values?
        1.
        2.
        3.
        4.
        5.

    b.   How might your values influence your everyday behavior? Do you encourage bullying behaviors?

    c.   How do you practice acts of kindness? (Give examples)

    d.   Name things you need to be happy, successful, or have a meaningful life?

        I need ...

    e.   Give an example of who you value and respect most and why?

    f.   How do you want to be remembered by others after high school? How do you think people perceive you now?

Activity #24: Student Confessions and Identifying Bullying Roles

Activity goal: For students to better understand who they are (either a bully, bystander, helper or target) according to their family background and personal experiences.

Approximate activity time: 45 minutes

Materials required: "Bullying Roles" printouts (*provided below*), *My Role in Bullying Confession* student worksheet

Step-by-step activity process:

N.B. This activity may be considered uncomfortable for some, so it is recommended to use a few sessions after the topic has been introduced and discussed.

1. Before the start of the activity, let students know that today you all will be discussing some personal experiences and issues. Let them know that for some, the topics might be uncomfortable but that they should, nevertheless, be open and honest about it as it will help a great deal in creating awareness around bullying as an issue.
2. Ask students:
    a. What is your role in bullying? Are you a bully, bystander, helper or target of bullying? Note that most people don't know what they are.
    b. What are some characteristics of a bully? (*E.g., he or she says or does hurtful things to others—online, text message, physical, verbal or nonverbal—purposely or unconsciously*)
    c. What are some characteristics of a target? (*E.g., he or she is shy, insecure, does not have many friends and different from the majority or popular group*)
    d. What are some characteristics of a bystander? (*E.g., he or she is a follower who watches others being made fun of or bullied*)
    e. What are some characteristics of a helper? (*E.g., he or she is brave, cool, loving, sensitive, caring and a leader*)

f. Go deeper/probe further.
   i. Ask: Where do you fit in?
   ii. Are you a: (a) bully, (b) bystander, (c) supporter or (d) target of bullying?
3. Put or stick the 4 "Bullying Roles" (*provided below*) in each corner of the room.
4. Ask students to move to the area of the room that corresponds to their character and sit together in a closed circle.
5. Next, distribute *My Role in Bullying Confession* student worksheet to each student.
   a. First, ask students to take a few minutes to draw symbols of their experiences that shaped their behavior, i.e., influences that might have shaped them being a bully, target or bystander.
   b. Review worksheet by reading "Students Confession of Bullying Roles Examples."
   c. Once you are done, have them complete the worksheet alone, then discuss their answers in small groups.
   d. Ask students to be as honest as possible because this is how they will all learn and grow.

Extra confession: Return to a larger group circle and have each student confess their role in bullying. Let this exercise be an eye-opening experience for all of us to grow and learn about ourselves.

More group confessions:

Have each group answer and present the following phrases:

Post-activity discussion questions:

1. How did you feel about this exercise in total?
2. Was this exercise difficult? Was it hard to admit the role you play?
3. Have you ever confessed your role in bullying?
4. How do you feel about your role?
5. What's going on in your life for you to act this way?
6. How has your ancestry or culture affected who you are today?
7. What did you learn about yourself?

8. What can you do to help others or be more satisfied with yourself as a person?
9. Do you want to tell the class anything?
10. What factors influence your behavior?

Key take-away message:

Admitting who we are is the first step to change. We are all inherently good and have the potential to be great people, but often we tend to follow the norm and let our emotions get in the way. When we are stressed or anxious about something in our lives, we tend to express our hurt onto others.

Encourage students to come to you if they want to report or talk about a problem they have.

PREVENTING BULLYING:
A Manual For Teachers In Promoting Global Educational Harmony

Copy, cut and distribute

Understanding Bullying Roles

We are ... _____ (bullying role)

We often ... (Examples of common behaviors)

We like to ... (examples of activities or personal characteristics)

We hope to ...

We need to ...

Students' Confession of Bullying Roles Examples

Example: I think I'm a bully because ...

- I copy my father who is aggressive and angry all the time when he is at home. He barely speaks to me. I feel angry that he is never home and let my anger out on others at school who are happier or weaker than me. I know it's wrong, but it helps me deal with my problems.
- I'm not pretty like most girls at school. So, I find something wrong with them and then feel superior. I sometimes agree with my friends who make fun of other girls. But when I'm alone, I regret what I say and know it is not how my mother raised me. She would always say, "Who do you think you are talking like that about other people?! God? You're not and should never judge anyone. But mom doesn't know how hard it is to survive in high school.
- I keep my head up and don't smile often. I protect myself so people don't disrespect me, my religion and nationality. I have a lot of pride and have seen a lot of pain in my family from different people who hurt them. So, I come off strong because I don't trust people at school. So yes, I look like a bully, but it's not the real me.

Example: I think I'm a bystander because ...

- I don't want to get involved in a bad situation or be the target. I'm the middle child and have always seen my older brother and younger, party-animal sister get in trouble. I was the responsive one in my parents' eyes. But really, I was doing and saying the same bad things but not getting caught because I was just too afraid of getting hurt. I've seen girls at school hit each other and I was there watching, doing nothing to stop them. She had guts that I didn't have. I live through the excitement and drama by being part of that group and being there for others. I play it safe and watch my mouth to not get too directly involved or at the center of attention.

- I don't want to be laughed at, so I don't draw too much attention to myself and hang out with people that are nice and don't want drama.

Example: I think I'm a target because …

- of my disability. People feel nervous when they see me or talk to me, so it's easier to just ignore me in their opinion, but it really hurts even more because I'm alone most of the time.
- I started dating someone in school and then everyone started gossiping about my personal life and ignoring me like I had the plague. Even my friends started excluding me and gave me bad looks. I wanted to die. Who would have known one decision would change my entire school life.
- I'm smaller than most guys and so they think it's funny to push me around in front of other people. They feel tougher than me and I hate them for that.

Example: I think I'm a helper because …

- Every time I see someone getting picked on, I feel sick. I am very empathetic and feel for them when they get bullied. I remember the people close to me that got extremely bullied and it sucked. Why should I let others go through what I did? Targets of bullying need support and brave people to stand up for them and what is right. I'm like social police force. Sometimes I think this may be none of my business, but it is my business. The target is my peer, my friend and a person in need. So, it is my business to step in. I wish so many others weren't afraid of facing the crowd or the bully. We are stronger than we know. My mom taught me that as a single mom.
- Every time people make racist or gay jokes, I say it's not funny. My uncle is gay, and I heard so much about the injustice he's been through. Someone must speak up for others who are oppressed. I would hope someone would do the same for me.

Role in Bullying Confession

Who do you think you are?

1. I think am a _____ because _____
   _____
   _____
   _____

2. A time I felt this way was when …
   _____
   _____
   _____

3. I felt _____ (adjective) in this bullying role. Now
   I feel _____ (adjective) in this present role.
   _____
   _____
   _____

4. Ways I can improve myself and my behavior is to …
   _____
   _____
   _____

5. What kind of person do you want to be?
   _____
   _____
   _____

6. How can you show this in school and at home?
   _____
   _____
   _____

Step 5: Eliminate the Motivation to Bully by Building Peer Relations

Helping students build peer relations is one of the secret ingredients to preventing bullying. When students feel and understand their similarities, they are less likely to bully one another. Therefore, helping students to get to know each other and find things in common can reduce the motivation to bully and segregate. Putting students into groups with peers they hardly know or have spoken to in great depth can enable students to be heard and accepted for who they really are, in hopes of creating bonds and understanding that they are more alike than unalike and struggling with similar insecurities and needs.

How do you build peer relationships? You play non-competitive sports, games and activities. Help students see commonalities and not their differences.

"As the popular saying goes, a family who prays together, stays together. Likewise, a family or classroom who plays together, stays together. The classroom is an extension of the family, therefore you must treat them as though they are your children." — Raju Ramanathan

Activity #25: The Masks We Wear!

<u>Activity goal:</u> To encourage students to identify the "social masks" they wear and to discuss why they feel the need to wear these masks. This activity will also allow them to express their insecurities and face who they really are behind these masks.

<u>Approximate activity time:</u> 45–60 minutes

<u>Materials required:</u> "My Social Mask" student worksheet printouts (*provided below*)

<u>Step-by-step activity process:</u>

1. Let students know that in this session, they will be talking about the perceptions that others have of them and how that compares to their self-perceptions.
2. Ask students: What is it really like to be you? What is your "social image" or "social mask"? How do people perceive you? Is it different from the way you see yourself?
   Give examples:
   a. People act or dress a certain way but really want to be themselves and feel comfortable being who they are, but they feel pressured to fit in and accepted by their peers.
   b. "I act like I'm tough and okay with my identity but really on the inside, I'm shy and just want to be accepted and left alone."
   c. I think people see me as _____ (happy go lucky, cool, athletic, popular, shy, passive, part of the "in-crowd")
3. Ask students: Why do we try to hide behind these masks? What are we afraid of? (E.g., rejection, gossip, being bullied, etc.)
4. Copy, cut and distribute "My Social Mask" student worksheet.
5. Give students about 5 minutes to complete the worksheet.
6. After completion, have students discuss as a whole class or in small groups.

Additional Activities
- Have students cut out and make a social mask that depicts themselves. Then have students present it. Further exploration could be to draw their "ideal selves."
- Draw a cartoon of their social selves and the "demons/ monsters" that attack their self-esteem and self-worth. Share pictures with a small group.
- Draw examples of the stereotypical masks people wear at school, at home, in the workplace, on TV and in the media. Discuss it with the whole class.

Post-activity discussion questions:
1. Do you think our clothes make a difference in how we are perceived by our peers and teachers?
2. Do you think having a school uniform or dress code is a good idea?
3. Are you the same for everyone?
4. Who do you act differently towards?
5. How do people view you? Who really sees you?
6. How do you view yourself, and how do you want to be perceived?
7. How do you want to be remembered after high school? What do you want to be remembered for?

Key take-away message:
It is important for us to take a closer look at ourselves and those around us. Really look at each other... everyone has beauty. Everyone has an incredible story behind their masks; a story we most likely couldn't fathom. They have an incredible story about their ancestors. We all come from different places. The reason why we wear social masks is for a sense of security and comfort, as we know the judgments that go along with the mask. Being unmasked is risky as it could possibly lead to being attacked or bullied. The problem with a social mask is that if you wear it too long, you become it when it's not really who you are. We must build confidence in ourselves and love ourselves for who we are. And in turn, we must try to love those around us for who they are. This is the only way we can all co-exist harmoniously within our communities and in the world at large.

CHRISTINA THEOPHILOS, M.ED. & RAJU RAMANATHAN, M.TECH

- -

My Social Mask

Name:_____

Write a word or phrase that describes your social mask.

For example:

My social mask represents someone who is strong / confident / happy / a jock / shy / introverted because I know this is what I must do to be popular.

If I take off my mask, I'm someone who is unsure of myself and angry at having to conform/act in a way that is socially acceptable to fit in.

My social mask is … _____
_____ because _____
_____ .

If I take off my mask, I'm someone who … _____
_____
_____
_____

- -

PREVENTING BULLYING:
A Manual For Teachers In Promoting Global Educational Harmony

Activity #26: Find Commonalities — "Find Someone Who…"

Name: _____

Directions: *Write the name of a different person in each box. Sit and "connect," making eye contact with this person by asking more related questions, until the instructor says to "switch" with someone new. Then, shake hands and say, "It was nice connecting with you."*

Has fallen asleep in class.	Has forgotten their project at home.	Has the same number of siblings as you do.	Has failed a test.
Enjoys the same music as you.	Knows someone with a mental "disability."	Likes the same tv show as you.	Has tried meditation.
Parents are happily married.	Has the same computer knowledge as you.	Loves McDonalds.	Feels the same way you do today.
Has lost their confidence at some point in time.	Speaks more than two languages.	Has lost a friend.	Their family immigrated here.

Find Someone Who …

Has travelled somewhere you have.	Loves the same food as you.	Has a similar taste in music as you.	Has had trouble in math.
Shares a similar ancestry as you.	Has a similar pet animal as you.	Shares your values about friendship.	Has been concerned about their weight or appearance.
Has tried yoga and understands the benefits.	Dances and sings when no one is watching.	Holds the same religious or nonreligious beliefs.	Loves school as much as you do.
Has similar stress related problems.	Has lost someone they loved.	Has yelled at their parents.	Has been hurt by a parent or sibling.

The goal is to "connect" with EVERYONE in class.

Activity #27: "If You Really Knew Me"

<u>Activity goal:</u> To help relationship building among students by having them share statements about themselves that perhaps others never knew.

<u>Approximate activity time:</u> 45 minutes

<u>Materials required:</u> *If You Really Knew Me* Student Worksheet (provided below)

<u>Step-by-step activity process:</u>

1. Let students know that this is a relationship-building activity involving a short game and a small group discussion, with the goal of identifying what they have in common with each other. Note that there are many different cliques and groups of friends at school according to their shared style, music, gender or sports. However, we are all the same with the same goals and desires. Most people have the same insecurities, family problems, self-esteem issues and romance problems and dislike studying.
2. Next, make a random group of 4–6 students with peers they normally don't hang out with.
3. Introduce the topic of bullying by stating: "So many people bully because they don't know each other or hear each other's stories. They judge people without knowing them or simply because they are different."
4. Explain the goal to the class, i.e., to:
   a. share who you are and be proud.
   b. get to know your peers better.
   c. find something you all have in common.
      (Acknowledge how you are more alike than unalike.)
5. Note that if they are honest about their responses, this activity will be wonderful and moving, but if they don't trust and simply say what they think is cool or stay in their comfort zone, nothing will happen, and no one will learn.

6. Encourage students to listen attentively, trust and not judge one another. *This is not about gossiping; this is about being friendly and acting as a part of a community. Can you do this?*
7. Note that you are a family, and sometimes life is difficult, especially during high school. We are here as everyone's support group. No one should go through their problems alone. The first step is really getting to know each other. The next step is having friends and supporters who can help you if you are ever in trouble or being bullied.
8. Copy, cut and distribute the *"If you really knew me..."* sheets to each student.
9. Give students 5 minutes to review, take notes and think of their answers. (You can play soft music in the background.)
10. Ask students to begin with an open mind and heart and desire to *really* meet new friends.
11. Walk around the room monitoring each group dynamic.
12. In the end, thank everyone for participating and contributing honest answers.

Post-activity discussion questions:

1. How did you like this exercise? What question was most difficult?
2. What new information did you learn about each other? Anything surprising?
3. What is one thing you all had in common with each other?
4. How do you feel now? How did you feel when you first sat down?
5. What did you learn about yourself?
6. Do you think you can talk or confide in your group if you were ever bullied?

Note the importance of getting to know each other before we judge each other. Never judge a book by its cover.

PREVENTING BULLYING:
A Manual For Teachers In Promoting Global Educational Harmony

<u>Key take-away message:</u>

Life is difficult. So, if we work together and get to know each other better, we can help each other in times of need. Nowadays, bullying and stress are everywhere. We need to be open, kind and loving to each other because everyone has a story and some pain or insecurity in their life. We shouldn't be quick to judge others without knowing what they've gone through, or where they come from. No one's life is perfect. It is important to understand and get to know each other. We must have compassion for one another and judge each other based on our inner qualities.

CHRISTINA THEOPHILOS, M.ED. & RAJU RAMANATHAN, M.TECH

If You Really Knew Me — Student Worksheet

<u>Complete the following sentences:</u>
"If you really knew me, you would know…"

1. That the best thing I have ever done is …

2. What brings me the most peace is …

3. One piece of good news from my life this week is …

4. My closest family member is my …

5. What I find most difficult about coming to school is …

6. What I like most about school is …

7. My role model is …

8. If I had three wishes, I would wish for …

9. The funniest thing I can remember happening is …

10. I am someone who is …

11. I am most grateful for …

Activity #28: Admit Your Mistakes and Apologize to Those You Hurt

<u>Activity goal:</u> To encourage students to admit their wrongdoings, understand their mistakes, get peer feedback and move forward. This activity takes significant courage amongst students, so they should be reminded to treat each other with respect and be empathetic of each other.

<u>Approximate activity time:</u> 45–60 minutes

<u>Materials required:</u> Paper, pencils, blackboard

<u>Step-by-step activity process:</u>

N.B. This activity may be considered uncomfortable for some, but if a few students admit their mistakes, there may be a chain reaction of openness.

Part 1 — Admitting Our Mistakes

1. Let students know that this activity is intended to allow them to open up and admit to any mistakes they might have made while receiving support from their peers.
2. Have students sit in a large circle OR in groups of 5–6 people.
3. Make sure each student has a sheet of paper and a pencil.
4. Warm-up: Ask students to describe what it means to make a mistake and do wrong to others. Give examples. (E.g., *lying, cheating on a test, gossiping about someone's personal life, insulting someone, writing hurtful things on their Facebook page, looking down on others different from you, etc.*)
5. Note that we are all human and all make mistakes. The emphasis is that it is important to admit our mistakes and make it part of our growth and healing so that we don't make the same mistakes again.
6. Write the following on the board, overhead or individual student papers:

> *Admitting our mistakes questions:*
>
> A. Three mistakes you have made or wrongs you have done to others. (Examples: physical, verbal, emotional, cyber.)
> B. Why did you do it? (Examples: power, bad joke, anger, revenge.)
> C. Why was it wrong? (Examples: unkind, insulting, rude, selfish)
> D. What did you do next? (Examples: apologize, walk away, cry, ignore it, get angry, insult yourself, blame yourself, forget about it, etc.)
> E. What did you learn about yourself from this mistake? (Example: I can be inconsiderate and hurt those I care about.)
> F. What can you do now to better yourself or the situation/relationship? (group feedback)

7. Leave students 10 minutes to complete the task.
8. After they have completed, ask students to share their answers in their small groups.
9. Thank all students for their participation.

Post-activity discussion questions:

1. How did you feel sharing your "wrongs and mistakes" with others?
2. Was it hard to trust them? Were you scared that they would judge you?
3. Do you feel a greater bond between your group members?
4. Did you gain any feedback?

Key take-away message:

Admitting our mistakes is the first step to change and better ourselves. Saying we are sorry is one of the hardest things to do, but one of the greatest signs of personal growth and maturity. In order to avoid having our problems or misinterpretations linger, we all must come to terms with our mistakes and find ways to resolve or amend them. Sometimes people don't know the impact of what they do or say, so it's important to express our pain and let the other person share his/her beliefs about a situation that could have been misinterpreted. This will help us grow and bring closure to the situation.

Encourage students to come to you if they want to report or talk about a problem they have.

Part 2: Apologizing to Those You Hurt

*** (same as other 3 sections, very delicate in nature)

Activity goal: For students to understand the greatness and courage of apologizing, in hopes that they can do the same to 3 people they have hurt/rejected/or insulted in their lives. Remember that this activity can be hard for some students. Encourage everyone to feel comfortable and remind them that their group will act as their support.

Approximate activity time: 60 minutes

Materials required: Apology Worksheet printouts (*provided below*), paper, and pencils

Step-by-step activity process:

N.B. *This activity may be considered uncomfortable for some, but if a few apologize, there may be an encouraging chain reaction.*

1. Introduce the activity by letting students know that this is an exercise in apologizing and asking for forgiveness for mistakes they have made or wrongs they have done. Remind them that this is an important step in their growth and maturity.
2. Divide the class into small groups of 4–5 students.
3. Make sure each student has a paper and a pencil.

4. Open the discussion with the following questions:
   a. Have you ever told anyone you were sorry? Think of a time you did. (Pause.)
   b. How did you apologize? Was it easy? Were you sincere in your apology? Did they forgive you easily? Why or why not?
   c. What is the best way to say sorry for hurting someone's feelings?
5. In groups, discuss the "Top 6 apologizing tips" and the reason for your answers. Tell students they will have 10–15 minutes to discuss and then present their ideas.
6. After completion, ask a few groups to share their responses.
7. Review key points when apologizing (see *"Tips for Teachers Use" below*).
8. Thank students for their efforts and discuss the importance of apologizing.
   Note that we are all human and we have all hurt others, consciously or inadvertently. Remind students that it is important to admit our mistakes, which is part of our growth and healing, so that we don't make the same mistakes again. It is important to be brave and say when you've done wrong and try not to do it again.
9. Next, now that they know how to apologize properly, ask students to return to their individual seats and think of 3 people whom they have hurt, and whom they would like to apologize to. (E.g., Gossiping about your best friend, yelling at your mother, ignoring someone in class, making fun of someone, etc.)

Post-activity discussion questions:

1. Describe how it feels to apologize and say sorry. (Examples: difficult, uncomfortable.)
2. Ask students how it feels to receive an apology. (Examples: relieved, happy, grateful.)
3. Was this activity helpful to you?
4. Do you forgive yourself more now that you apologized?

PREVENTING BULLYING:
A Manual For Teachers In Promoting Global Educational Harmony

<u>Key take-away message:</u>

People who don't apologize are the ones who live with the most guilt and regret. It is important to acknowledge our mistakes, ask for forgiveness, and forgive others who have hurt us. Encourage students to come to you if they want to report or talk about a problem they have.

Example: Corrie Ten Boom, a woman who survived a Nazi concentration camp during the Holocaust, said, "Forgiveness is to set a prisoner free, and to realize the prisoner was you."

We are the ones who suffer most when we choose not to forgive. When we do forgive our hearts become free from anger, bitterness, resentment and hurt that previously imprisoned us.

Student Worksheet

Top 6 apologizing tips:	Reasoning
1.	1._____ _____
2.	2._____ _____
3.	3._____ _____
4.	4._____ _____
5.	5._____ _____
6.	6._____ _____

Tips for Teachers' Use:

1. Find the right time to apologize (cool-down period; the sooner the better).
2. Write out your apology as a letter for practice or a back-up plan if it gets too difficult.
3. Speak sincerely.
4. Be specific and say exactly what you said or did wrong.
5. Explain that you did not mean to hurt them.
6. Take full responsibility for your actions.
7. Do not give excuses.
8. Avoid phone calls and text messages while you are apologizing (it is less sincere and personal).
9. State what you said or did and the resulting feelings you may have caused. Explain why you did or said what you did.
10. Promise that you hope to avoid making the mistake again in the future.
11. Express your appreciation of the relationship you have with the person and that you don't want to damage it.
12. Be patient and stick to your word.

Apology Worksheet

Complete the following apology questions and tasks:

1. Write down 2 hurtful things you've done to people at school. (*For example, hurt means insulted, pushed, embarrassed, rejected, gossiped about, looked down upon, etc.*)

    a. What you did: _____

       Person A: _____

    b. What you did: _____

       Person B: _____

2. Write 1 hurtful thing you've done to a family member.

    a. What you did: _____

       Person C: _____

3. Write notes below on how you can apologize and how you feel (using what you learned in the top 6 apologizing tips).
4. Apologize either in person or by letter or phone.
   <u>Post-apology questions</u> (next class discussion):
    a. How was your apologizing experience?

    b. How did the person react?

    c. How did you feel during and/or after the apology?

    d. Did the person forgive you?

    e. What did you learn about yourself?

EXTRA:

Student apology activity (modified):

- Think of 3 people in the class you may have been mean to.
- Go up to them, say "Sorry," and explain your thoughts and reasons when you are feeling full of peace, bravery, and readiness.
- Give examples (not sharing your food or pencils, not being their friend or playing basketball with them, and so on).
- Forgiveness: What is it? Do you forgive yourself and others who have hurt you?
- How do you all feel now?

Christina Theophilos, M.Ed. & Raju Ramanathan, M.Tech

I'm sorry. Please forgive me. Thank you and love you.
— Inspired from the Ho'oponopono Prayer

Apology Letter

An apology is an expression of remorse or guilt over having said or done something that is acknowledged to be hurtful, and a request for forgiveness.

Dear _____,

What you did:

How you feel:

What you promise:

What you value:

Final words:

Signed,

PREVENTING BULLYING:
A Manual For Teachers In Promoting Global Educational Harmony

EXTRA HOMEWORK ASSIGNMENT:

Writing an apology: Name:
_____
_____
_____

What did you do or say?
_____
_____
_____

Who did you say it to and why?
_____
_____
_____

How did you feel after?
_____
_____
_____

What do you want them to know now?
_____
_____
_____

What did you learn from this experience?
_____
_____
_____

Signature:

Activity #29: Share Your Bullying Story and Let It Go

This activity may be difficult for students and may even generate emotions and inner conflicts when sharing intense personal stories (class judgment must not be present).

Activity goal: For all students to share a personal story of being bullied. This process will build a sense of togetherness and mutual understanding and act as a support group. This will also help them get feedback, encouragement, self-understanding and healing in a supportive community.

Audience: late elementary or high school students

Approximate activity time: 45–60 minutes

Materials required: Bullying questions (*provided below*)

Step-by-step activity process:

1. Explain to students that this activity is aimed at bringing them closer together as a group and will entail requiring them to share personal stories and be open and honest with each other.
2. Ask the class to discuss what "bullying" means. Ask students to give examples (if it hasn't been covered already).
3. Write (a) verbal, (b) physical, and (c) online bullying on the board or overhead projector.
4. Ask students to give examples of each type of bullying.
5. Ask students to *raise their hands* if they have ever been a target of bullying.
6. Tell them that they will be sharing their stories today for their personal healing.
7. After a few suggestions, divide students into groups of 3–4 students.
8. Copy, cut and distribute the questions provided below to each student or one copy per group.
9. Read the questions and give an example that you can relate to.

10. Ask students to share their stories of a bullying experience they have experienced or witnessed that still might bother them.
11. Note that we learn from each other's experiences, building friendships, and can be a support group for each other. Ask that students <u>listen carefully</u> to their peers, and leave ample time for each student to share their story. Remind the class that almost everyone has a story about bullying and here is a chance to let it go and <u>practice giving positive and supportive feedback</u> after they do.
12. **Option 1:** Allow all students to write their bullying experiences on a scrap sheet of paper, and after they are done sharing, to throw the paper in the garbage (placed in the center of the room) like a burning ceremony, which some Native Indian communities do. Play some tribal, Zen, or soothing music in the background to create this "letting go of hurtful past experiences."

    Extra: find or create a "Native Talking Stick" to enable the person in each group to have permission to speak without interruption.
13. Leave students at least 15–20 minutes to complete the task. Thank students for their openness and honesty.

<u>Sharing bullying stories:</u>

1. Have you ever been bullied verbally, physically or online?
2. If so, tell your group about what happened. (Not too lengthy so everyone has time to share their stories.)
3. How did you feel? What did you do afterwards?
4. If you could turn back time, what would you change?
5. Why is it important to "let go" and forget about this experience?
6. What did you learn about yourself and others from this experience?

    *Supportive and encouraging group feedback time!

<u>Post-activity discussion questions:</u>

1. How did you feel sharing your bullying experiences with others?
2. Was it nice to hear others' experiences?
3. Do you feel a greater bond between your group members?

4. What feedback did you receive?

<u>Key take-away message:</u>

Everyone has been bullied in some way, shape or form. It's important to talk about it with others and sometimes difficult (for boys, especially) since it involves expressing their feelings. Take the time to always learn from your experiences and do better from them.

Encourage students to come to you if they want to report or talk about a problem they have.

Activity #30: Forgive Vs. Holding Grudges

Activity goal: For students to understand and define the value of forgiveness, in the hope that they can do the same to 3 people who have hurt, rejected or insulted them. This is part of the growth and maturity process established in some of the earlier activities and should be conducted after the apology activities.

Approximate activity time: 30 minutes

Materials required: *"Understanding Forgiveness"* student worksheet printouts (*provided below*)

Step-by-step activity process:

1. Let students know that in this session, they will understand the importance that forgiveness plays in making amends and moving on.
2. Ask students to break into small groups of 3 or 4 students.
3. Copy and distribute the *"Understanding Forgiveness"* sheet (*provided below*).
4. Ask students to discuss and write the answers to the "Understanding Forgiveness" questions.
5. Ask students to share some of their answers with the rest of the class.
6. After completion, thank students for their participation.

Post-activity discussion questions:

1. What did you learn from this activity?
2. Why is forgiveness important?
3. How does it feel to forgive others? How does it feel to forgive yourself? Which one is more important?
4. Was this helpful?
5. Do you forgive yourself more now that you apologized?

Key take-away message:

We all make mistakes, and learning from them is part of our growth process. Forgiveness is also a part of the same process, as it helps us make amends and move past unhealthy situations. Understanding the value of forgiveness and utilizing this learning is what can help us grow and get stronger. At some time or another, we all get hurt. It is our choice to forgive and forget or allow the situation/incident to leave a mark and negatively impact our future. Holding onto grudges and ill feelings towards someone can influence our daily lives, making it difficult for us to move past painful experiences and really live our lives to the fullest. People who don't forgive have much greater stress levels and anger and less overall inner happiness. We must all aim to live happier lives, and as part of that effort, we must understand and practice the act of forgiveness.

Encourage students to come to you if they want to report or talk about a problem they have.

Tips for teachers on forgiveness:

What is forgiveness?	**What are the effects of holding a grudge?**
Forgiveness ...	If you're unforgiving:
• Is letting go of resentment and thoughts of revenge. • Helps you focus on other parts of your life instead of the painful ones. • Helps you understand others, feel empathy and compassion to those who hurt you.	• You may feel constant anger and bitterness in every relationship and new experience. • Your life may become so wrapped up in the wrong that you can't enjoy the present. • You may become depressed or anxious. • You may feel that your life lacks meaning or purpose. • You may lose valuable and enriching connectedness with others.
What are the benefits of forgiving someone?	
• Feeling more peace and less resentment, sadness, and anger • Feeling happier and less depressed • Having healthier and better relationships • Gaining greater spiritual and psychological well-being • Less stress • Lower blood pressure • Lower risk of alcohol and substance abuse	**How do I reach a state of forgiveness?** • Forgiveness is a commitment to a process of change. Forgiveness goes against our nature; we must forgive by faith, whether we feel like it or not. • Recognize the value of forgiveness and its importance in your life at a given time. • Then, reflect on the facts of the situation, how you've reacted, and how this combination has affected your life, health and well-being.

Why do people hold grudges?	• When you're ready, actively choose to forgive the person who offended you.
• When you're hurt by someone you love and trust, you may become angry, sad or confused. If you dwell on hurtful events or situations, grudges filled with resentment, vengeance, and hostility may take root. If you allow negative feelings to crowd out positive feelings, you may find yourself swallowed up by your own bitterness or sense of injustice. *Just let it go.*	• Move away from your role as a target and release the control and power the offending person and situation have had in your life. • As you let go of grudges, you'll no longer define your life by how you've been hurt. • You may even find compassion and understanding.

PREVENTING BULLYING:
A Manual For Teachers In Promoting Global Educational Harmony

Student Worksheet: Heal and Grow Through Forgiveness

<u>*Understanding Forgiveness*</u>

1. What is forgiveness?
2. What are the benefits of forgiving someone who hurt you? (name at least 4)

    a. a.

    b. b.

    c. c.

    d. d.

    Other:

3. Why do people hold grudges?

4. What are the 3 negative effects of holding a grudge against someone who hurt you?

5. Give 2 examples of people who have hurt or bullied you:
    Person A: _____ (story)

    Person B: _____ (story)

6. Did you forgive them? If so, how?

7. If you have not forgiven them, how can you try?

Step 6: Provide Opportunities to Practice Conflict Resolution and Interpersonal Skills

"Compassionate education" is a term used to define ways that teachers can help alter how students see others and themselves. In order to do so, teachers must give them a series of thought-provoking inner values, and how their actions are aligned with these compassionate values that they know and hold to be true, but often neglect to apply.

Therefore, this chapter will help students practice their compassionate skills and behaviors using role-play exercises, debates and more, including a powerful complimenting exercise that will help build bonds and say the things we really should be saying to each other.

Imagine students who can't concentrate in class due to getting bullied feeling calmer and more secure in your class. Targets of bullying no longer feel afraid of walking through the halls or on the bus. Imagine every student coming to school with confidence, reassurance, and a smile on their face, willing and wanting to be there and learn.

"The way to resolve conflict in groups, is by dropping the conflict within you.

No matter what the age group your students are, your inner vibration and the way you relate to their higher self should be the same. When I look at children, I look at their future avatar." — Raju Ramanathan

The S.T.O.P. Technique for Conflict Resolution

S -	*Stop and take a moment to center yourself.*
T -	*Tune into your own higher vibration of love and acceptance.*
O -	*Observe your breath, feelings, and still-point within yourself. Next, observe your students as beautiful souls, not rascals.*
P -	*Perceive new possibilities of positive behavior and visualize your students having a great time with you and each other's presence.*

It does not matter WHAT you communicate, it matters only where you communicate from within yourself. It does not matter what you say, what matters is, HOW you say it." — Raju Ramanathan

Activity #31: Locating Bullying Hot Spots and How to Respond

Activity goal: For students to identify where bullies tend to bully their targets (e.g., "hot spots," location and prevention tactics).

This activity is recommended after a few discussions or activities on bullying.

Approximate activity time: 30–45 minutes

Materials required: School map—photocopies to distribute or large print to show as display or projector display; *"Locating Bullying Hot Spots"* prints (*provided below*)

Step-by-step activity process:

1. Introduce the activity to students by letting them know that they will be talking about and identifying "hot spots" of bullying— i.e., common places that bullies might choose to victimize their targets.
2. Draw or find a copy of a map of the school. Either distribute photocopies, display on the overhead projector or display a large print for all the class to see. *Note: If school map is not available, then draw a rough outline of the school on the blackboard.*
3. Divide the class into groups of 4–5 students.
4. Copy the *"locating bullying hot spots"* form and distribute to each group (*see below*).
5. Leave about 15 minutes for each group to complete the questions.
6. After completion, ask each group to present their answers.
7. Thank the class for their participation.

Extra: Give each group a "bullying hotspot" or location (see below) and ask them to think of a bullying scenario. Ask students to make a short skit showing what students can do to defend themselves in this situation and location.

PREVENTING BULLYING:
A Manual For Teachers In Promoting Global Educational Harmony

Bullying Hot Spots:

Group 1) Hallways or stairwells

Group 2) Bathrooms

Group 3) On the bus or at the bus stop

Group 4) Locker rooms

Group 5) Cafeteria

Group 6) Outside hang out area or playground

Post-activity discussion questions:

1. Where do bullies hang out? How do you know? Have you ever witnessed it? What did you do?
2. Where do bullies usually target their target(s)? Where is the "hottest" or most common spot and why?
3. Do girls and boys bully in the same place?
4. Do you think bullies prefer to pick on others "in public" or "in private?"
5. Why do you think bullies prefer humiliating others in public?
6. Who do they usually bully? (Examples: people different from them, those with not many friends, etc.)
7. Do bullies pick on people of the same or of different genders?
8. What can targets do to protect themselves in these "hot spots?"
9. What can all students realistically do to make these "hot spots" feel safer?
10. What can the school or adults do to help keep these "hotspots" safe? (Examples: monitor, camera, posters?)
11. Would you feel safer if extra precaution was taken to monitor these "hot spots?" If not, why?

Key take-away message:

The focus of this activity is to help students identify the hotspots and discuss ways in which one can avoid these areas or take action against making these bullying locations. Students need to be reminded to show confidence at all times to ensure they don't become a target of bullying, especially in and around these hotspots.

Reinforce how students should act when confronted by a bully or bullying situation: **smile and walk away, tell them to STOP in a calm and assertive manner, don't show your pain, use humor, walk with friends, exercise, join martial arts, make new friends and report the bullying.** Let the bully know it's not cool to bully others. Be leaders, step up and stop the abuse! Or find a new, safer and cooler place to hang. (Don't forget outside of school, hallways, bathroom, bus stops, and school buses).

Encourage students to come to you if they want to report or talk about a problem they have.

PREVENTING BULLYING:
A Manual For Teachers In Promoting Global Educational Harmony

Locating Bullying Hot Spots

Copy, cut and distribute.

---

1. Draw the school layout and make happy faces where it's safe for all students to hang out. ☺

   Write the locations here:
   _____
   _____

   What makes these places safe for students to hang out there?
   _____

2. Put an X where it's common for students to be bullied or where fights are.
   Write the places here:
   _____
   _____

   What are some reasons why it isn't safe for targets in this area?
   _____
   _____

3. Where do *you* hang out? Have you ever been bullied there?
   _____
   _____

4. What are some characteristics of the people bullies usually pick on?
   _____
   _____

5. How do you think targets of bullying feel after they have been humiliated or abused publicly?
   _____
   _____

6. What can targets do in these unavoidable "hot spots" in order to stop or prevent bullying?
   _____
   _____

7. Do your friends bully or make fun of others? Have you ever tried to stop them?
   _____
   _____

8. What are two actions someone can do if they witness bullying?
   _____
   _____

9. What can targets do to (a) *defend or stand up* and (b) *feel better* about themselves?
   _____
   _____

PREVENTING BULLYING:
A Manual For Teachers In Promoting Global Educational Harmony

Locating Bullying Hot Spots: Teacher's Answer Sheet

For Teacher's Use only

1. Draw the school layout and make happy faces where it's safe for all students to hang out. ☺
   Write the locations here:

   Anywhere there is supervision or an adult who can punish/scold them. (inferior: age, social status)

   What makes these places safe for students to hang out there?

   Adult supervision, sanctions

2. Put an X where it's common for students to be bullied or where fights are.
   Write the places here:

   Hallways, bathrooms, stairwells, buses, bus stops, locker rooms, cafeteria and playgrounds

   What are some reasons why it isn't safe for targets in this area?

   Lack of supervision from adults or people of authority

3. Where do *you* hang out? Have you ever been bullied there?

4. What are some characteristics of the people bullies usually pick on?

   Shy, quiet, introverted, not many friends, different; color, sexual orientation, nationality, fashion/clothes, religion, ability, interests, rumors, height, weight, glasses, braces, hair, speech, accent, sports, athletic ability, financial / social status, opinion, life choices (e.g., not to smoke or drink) ... anything they can find to humiliate and have power over.

5. How do you think targets of bullying feel after they have been humiliated or abused publicly?

Sick, ill, nervous, anxious, depressed, suicidal, lonely, angry, revengeful, hurt, alone, afraid, unhappy, ashamed, unmotivated, low self-worth and esteem, that they are to blame and insignificant ... lifelong trauma.

6. What can targets do in these unavoidable "hot spots" in order to stop or prevent bullying?

7. Do your friends bully or make fun of others? Have you ever tried to stop them?

8. What are two actions someone can do if they witness bullying?

   A. Spread the word that bullying isn't cool. It won't be long before everyone agrees.
   B. Walk away instead of standing and watching bullying. Don't encourage it. Go get someone to help (like a nice senior or teacher).
   C. Tell the bully that their actions are wrong. And that they should go see a counselor if they seek attention. Don't take it out on others.
   D. Help the person being bullied by talking to them and telling them it's going to get better. Then report it to a parent, teacher or counselor.
   E. Refuse to hang out with people who are mean to others.

9. What can targets do to (a) *defend* or *stand up* and (b) *feel better* about themselves?
   - **Act confident.** Stand up straight, speak clearly and look secure even if you aren't. Make the person think they are not bothering you and they are wasting their time trying to tease you.
   - **Stay calm, don't say anything nasty or act offended or angry.** This is probably what the person bullying wants you to do.

PREVENTING BULLYING:
A Manual For Teachers In Promoting Global Educational Harmony

- **Keep your words simple.** Don't get too wordy or emotional. Be assertive, and then walk away. Ignore what the bully will say next to try and get the last word.
- **Show that you don't care by saying things like:**
    - "I don't care what you think."
    - "I'm not really interested."
    - "Who cares?."
    - "So?"
- **Make a joke and say:**
    - "I love you too!"
    - "You're so lovable!"
    - "You're so wonderful!"
    - "Thank you, have a nice day!"
    - "Wow, that was so nice of you!"
- **Calmly remove yourself from the situation.** Say your piece, then walk away or ignore the bullying by turning and walking away calmly and confidently.
- **If they try to stop or block you.** Be firm and clear —look them in the eye and tell them to stop.
- **Don't fight back.** If you fight back you could make the situation worse, get hurt or be blamed for starting the trouble. "An eye for an eye makes everyone blind." — Gandhi
- **Take a martial arts or self-defense class** if physical abuse continues. You can also study some blocking positions online. Practice with a friend or family member so you can be prepared for an attack.
- **Get away from the situation** as quickly as possible and go cool down somewhere.
- **Go tell an adult** what has happened straight away. **Don't be afraid** to talk to an adult you trust (like your teacher, counselor or your parent). Brainstorm solutions or interventions together. Keep talking to them until the bullying has stopped.
- **Tell a friend about it.** Try to avoid being alone in places the bully may pick on you. Go where there are plenty of people and ask a friend(s) to go with you. Stay or act calm and practice

what you can do the next time if the bullying happens again. Remember that bullies usually want a negative reaction from you.
- **Think positively**—remember you are a good person. Remind yourself of your strengths and the things you are good at and that it will get easier. We all have a purpose in life and these experiences will make us stronger and enable us to help others who have experienced pain.
- **Attend youth or religious centers** (e.g., church, synagogue, mosque or temple or a youth group where you can talk to people, meet new friends, get support and pray about your situation. This is another effective way to gain strength, wisdom and inner peace.)
- **On the school bus,** try to sit near the driver and talk to the people around you. If it's an ordinary city bus, sit near an adult.
- **Walking home.** If you have to walk home and you're afraid of being ambushed, try taking different routes, try to leave home and school a bit later or a bit earlier, or see if you can walk with other people who live near you, even if they're older or younger.

Activity #32: Improvise Bullying Response Strategies

Activity goal: It is often easy to suggest what one can do in a bullying situation but much harder to react in that manner when faced with such a situation. Role-playing activities help place students in the shoes of a bully or target and encourage them to experiment with different behaviors and solutions prior to using them in a real-life scenario. This also allows them to test out what reactions/actions they are comfortable with when confronted with a bullying situation.

The material to accompany each episode/webisode presents a series of role- play scenarios using characters from the episode.

Approximate activity time: 30–45 minutes

Materials required: None

Step-by-step activity process:

1. Let students know that in this activity they will be role-playing different bullying scenarios.
2. Encourage students to RECOGNIZE, REACT and RESPOND to bullying. This entails having students instinctively respond to bullying the right way for the benefit of everyone. This also involves reporting the bully to authorities who can help put a stop to the bullying.
3. Ask students to take their chairs and make a large circle, while making room in the center for the improvisation scenes.
4. Ask for or randomly select 3 people to act out each role and give the best possible solutions to each bullying scenario. *Optional:* Divide students into groups and give them time to prepare their short skits.
5. Tell them that they should do their best to practice defending one another in order to be prepared if they ever witness or experience bullying.

6. Ask them to share the most common types of bullying. Mark them on the board and then proceed to having students act out the best responses.
7. Congratulate and appreciate their efforts.

<u>Post-activity discussion questions:</u>

1. What do you think the purpose of this activity was?
2. What did you enjoy the most from this session?
3. What else did you learn from this activity?
4. What was most difficult for you during this activity?
5. Can you suggest ways of improving this activity?

PREVENTING BULLYING:
A Manual For Teachers In Promoting Global Educational Harmony

Bullying Scenarios

Cut, copy and distribute to each group.

What would you do if ...:

1. ... you saw someone getting pushed in gym class?

2. ... you received a threatening email from someone?

3. ... you saw someone who was short getting picked on?

4. ... you saw someone getting their lunch money stolen?

5. ... you saw someone getting ridiculed and pushed on the bus?

6. ... you saw someone sitting alone in the lunchroom?

7. ... you saw someone being rejected by their group of friends?

8. ... you heard someone being put down by others?

9. ... you heard a racist comment? (Possible response: "STOP! That's a racist comment and I want you to stop.")

10. ... you heard a joke about LGBTQ people?

Activity #33: Brainstorm Anti-Bullying Responses in Small Groups

Activity goal: To have students read and discuss bullying scenarios in small groups and then share their responses with the class. These examples will teach students how it feels to be picked on, in hopes of teaching empathy and conflict resolution.

Approximate activity time: 30 minutes

Materials required: *"In-class Bullying Scenarios"* sheet (*provided below*)

Step-by-step activity process:

1. Inform students that in this session, they will talk about different situations that a target of bullying can face and how someone can respond to those situations.
2. Divide the class into random groups of 4–5 students.
3. Copy, cut and distribute a *"Bullying Scenario"* to each group. (*See below.*)
4. Ask students to read the scenario and answer the following questions:
   a. How does the student (target) in the scenario feel?
   b. How does the bully / do the bullies feel?
   c. How do the bystanders feel?
   d. What can the target *realistically* do in response?
   e. What are 3 reasons why students shouldn't partake in this bullying behavior?

5. Once complete, ask each group to present their scenario and answers. Thank students for their ideas and participation.

PREVENTING BULLYING:
A Manual For Teachers In Promoting Global Educational Harmony

<u>Post-activity discussion questions:</u>

1. What do you think the purpose of this activity was?
2. What did you *learn about yourself* from this activity? Have you ever experienced any of these bullying examples? Did you report them to or tell someone about it that could help the target?
3. Do you really practice the phrase, "Treat others the way you want to be treated?"

<u>Key take-away message:</u>

Targets of bullying can be targeted for various reasons. Students must learn to appreciate diversity and learn to value the uniqueness that is in each of us. Reinforce that bullying affects everyone.

In-class Bullying Scenarios

Cut, copy and distribute to each group.

Scenario A

Students in class often laugh and ignore what a student says because he or she is in the "uncool" gang.

    a. How does the student (target) in the scenario feel?
    b. How does the bully / do the bullies feel?
    c. How do the bystanders feel?
    d. What can the target *realistically* do in response?

Scenario B

Students in class excluded a girl because of a rumor they heard.

    a. How does the student (target) in the scenario feel?
    b. How does the bully / do the bullies feel?
    c. How do the bystanders feel?
    d. What can the target *realistically* do in response?

Scenario C

The class bully said, "I don't want to work with _____ , he/she is an idiot."

    a. How does the student (target) in the scenario feel?
    b. How does the bully/do the bullies feel?
    c. How do the bystanders feel?
    d. What can the target *realistically* do in response?

PREVENTING BULLYING:
A Manual For Teachers In Promoting Global Educational Harmony

Scenario D
When the teacher wasn't looking, the group of students began throwing papers and erasers behind the head of a class target.

    a.   How does the student (target) in the scenario feel?

    b.   How does the bully/do the bullies feel?
    c.   How do the bystanders feel?
    d.   What can the target *realistically* do in response?

Scenario E

Extra:

Activity #34: Practice Makes Perfect — More Bullying Scenarios

Activity goal: Another activity to encourage empathy among students for targets of bullying via role-playing exercises. This activity asks students to think of solutions to the given bullying scenarios. (*Optional: have students act out the bullying scenario.*)

Approximate activity time: 45 minutes

Materials required: *"Bullying Scenarios"* sheet (*provided below*); *"Best Response"* worksheet (*provided*); prizes if awarded to the best group effort

Step-by-step activity process:

1. Introduce the activity by letting students know that they will be given certain bullying-related scenarios and asked to find appropriate solutions for them.
2. Divide the class into groups of 3–5 students
3. Distribute scenario sheet (see below).
4. Ask each group to read the scenarios then find solutions for the target and bystanders. Distribute *"The Best Responses"* worksheet.
5. Once all the groups have finished, ask them to present their "best responses."
   Extra: The group that found the best and most realistic responses wins a prize (e.g., candy, pencils), or have each group act out the best anti-bullying scenario.
6. After completion, thank all students for their participation.
7. Homework assignment: Distribute *"Best Response to Bullying: Student worksheet"* for further learning.

Post-activity discussion questions:

1. Which team had the best responses, and why?
2. What else can bystanders do to prevent or stop bullying?
3. What else can targets do?

4. Which is the worst form of bullying, scenario A, B, C, or D? Why?
5. What did you learn from this activity?
6. What else can you do to prevent bullying?
7. Did you enjoy this activity?

<u>Key take-away message:</u>

We have a responsibility to ourselves and others to make our environment safe for all and nurture a culture of community and togetherness. Remind students to always speak to a trusted authority figure if faced with a bullying situation because no one deserves to go through this alone.

Cut, copy and distribute to each group.

Bullying Scenarios

<u>Directions:</u> In groups, read each bullying scenario. Discuss, brainstorm and write the best possible responses that the target can do on a separate sheet of paper. Each group will then present their answers.

A) cyber abuse

> He wrote that I looked like a loser on my Facebook profile picture and a few people wrote that they agreed, laughed or "liked" his comment. I was horrified.

B) social abuse

> Tina turned all my friends against me because of a silly disagreement we had. She told hurtful things about me that were untrue. I was shocked when most of my long-time good friends took her side and started ignoring me when they saw me. During lunch, I didn't know where to sit because I usually sat with Tina and my friends.

C) verbal abuse

> Each time I walk by Joe, he begins to imitate and try to speak in my native language. It sounds ridiculous and everyone begins to laugh except me and my two good friends.

D) sexual abuse

> I was date-raped at a party and the guy told everyone I was a whore and sucked in bed. I was so embarrassed that I cried for hours when my best friend told me he said that to people.

PREVENTING BULLYING:
A Manual For Teachers In Promoting Global Educational Harmony

---

E) physical abuse

Each time I walk by Moe, he purposely and forcefully pumps into me and laughs with his friends.

F) non-verbal abuse

When the teacher says to work in groups during class, everyone just turns their backs on me and ignores me when I try to make eye contact or talk to them.

G) verbal abuse

Every time I change in the dressing room before gym class, ____ _____ (name of bully) loudly calls me a dyke or fag.

Activity #35: Time to Debate Bullying Topics

Activity goal: To introduce students to some basic concepts and terms on debating and have an informal debate on topics related to bullying. Debating classes are highly inclusive, which encourages teamwork, critical thinking and research. Students also enhance their public speaking skills, attentiveness and assertiveness.

Approximate activity time: 60+ minutes, including preparation and presentation time (could also be conducted as a homework assignment for debate research and preparation, with a 60-minute session for presentation).

Materials required: *"Bullying Debating Topics"* printouts (*provided below*); debating podium (if available); "speaking stick" if Option 2 is selected; *agree/disagree* signs if Option 3 is selected (*provided below*).

Step-by-step activity process:

Choose from one of the debating styles below based on your class.

Option 1: Formal Debate

1. Introduce the activity by letting students know that they will be practicing their debating skills, which will help improve their public speaking skills and their ability to be more assertive.
2. Divide the class into debate teams of 2 or 4 students.
3. Explain or review a debate process. (See Generic Debate Format example.)
4. Copy, cut and distribute or share the list of *"Bullying Debating Topics."*
5. Ask students to choose a debate topic or randomly assign one to each team.
6. Assign teams that will compete against each other. For example:
   a. Team 1: Affirmative/Government/Pros (Bullying is a learned behavior)

b. Team 2: Negative/Opposition/Cons, opposing the proposition (Bullying is an innate behavior)
7. Tell each group to prepare a 2-minute speech to support their argument/rationale. You can set this as either a homework assignment or after they prepare for 10–15 minutes in class.
8. Set up the layout for debate. Have the rest of the class (audience) sit behind the judges. *(See example layout provided below.)*
9. Assign 3–5 judges from opposite groups who will decide on the winning team based on the best and strongest arguments.
10. Assign a timekeeper to keep track of each speaker's 2-minute time limit.
11. Assign a chairperson (moderator or teacher) to introduce each topic, call on each participant and announce the winning team.
12. After the debate, thank all students for their participation.

Example of a typical debate room layout:

Option 2: Entire Class Debate (Less Formal)

1. Introduce the activity by letting students know that they will be practicing their debating skills which will help improve their public speaking skills and their ability to be more assertive.
2. Divide the class into 2 teams.
   a. Team 1: Affirmative/Government/Pros
   b. Team 2: Negative/Opposition/Cons, opposing the proposition
3. Assign judges or have the teacher be the judge according to how many supporting arguments were made. Make a point system on the board.
4. Share a debating topic and 10–15 minutes of group preparation (or assign preparation and research as a homework assignment).
5. Assign a chairperson (moderator or teacher) to introduce each topic, call on each participant and announce the winning team.
6. Begin casual debate, having students raise their hand or a "speaking stick" to speak.
7. After the debate, thank all students for their participation.

Option 3: Game-like Activity Using Debate Topics (casual format)

1. Introduce the activity by letting students know that they will be practicing their debating skills, which will help improve their public speaking skills and their ability to be more assertive.
2. Post the "Agree/Disagree" signs on opposite sides of the room.
3. Introduce the debating topics one at a time.
4. Have students cross the room and explain their opinion.
5. After the debate, thank all students for their participation.

Post-activity discussion questions:

1. What did you learn about bullying from this debate?
2. What was the strongest point made from this debate?
3. What did you learn about your own beliefs?
4. What new information was learned?
5. What (or who) did you most agree or disagree with most? Why?
6. How do you think this activity helps you in dealing with bullying?

Key take-away message:

Remind students that proper communication is important in any discussion or conflict. People disagree on many issues based on their own experiences, upbringing and values. It is important to communicate effectively and with an open mind and be willing to learn something new.

PREVENTING BULLYING:
A Manual For Teachers In Promoting Global Educational Harmony

Generic Debate Format

- There are two sides in a debate, known as the ***Affirmative*** (or *Government*) and the ***Negative*** (or *Opposition*). The terms *pro* and *con* and *for* and *against* often come up here.
- The subject to be discussed is known as the *resolution* (the most used term), the *proposition*, the *Bill*, the *measure* or the *issue*. Your students will probably think of others.
- Resolutions are, in Parliamentary debate, preceded by the expression "Be It Resolved That (or B.I.R.T.)." Examples:

QUESTION	RESOLUTION
Are these the best of all times?	B.I.R.T. these are the best of all times.
Are women better than men?	B.I.R.T. women are better than men.

1. There is a *resolution* of policy or value that provides the basic substance of the discussion. The terms of this resolution will be defined by the first speaker of the debate.
2. There are two teams representing those in favor of the resolution (*Government* or *Affirmative*) and those against (*Opposition* or *Negative*).
3. The Government/Affirmative always has the burden to prove its side.
4. The debate closes with final rebuttals on both sides, which summarize their respective positions.

1st Affirmative 2 min	1st Negative 2 min	2nd Affirmative 2 min	2nd Negative 2 min	Break 2 min	Neg Rebuttal & Summary 2 min	Affirmative Rebuttal & Summary 2 min

Notes on debating retrieved from http://www.csdf-fcde.ca/english/resources/NLSDU Teachers Guide to Debate.pdf.

Bullying Debate Topics

Cut, copy and explain to each group.

Have students find at least 3 supporting arguments, facts, definitions or statistics needed to help support their argument. What are the pros and cons of this argument? What are the problems and what are some alternatives? What is your team's plan of action to help support your side?

QUESTION	RESOLUTION
A. Should bullying be considered a crime?	A. Bullying should be considered a crime even in high school.
B. Should cyberbullying be punished at school?	B. Cyberbullying should be sanctioned on school grounds.
C. Can bullying build your character?	C. Bullying builds character and will make a target stronger.
D. Is fighting/hitting back the best solution?	D. Fighting back is the best solution for bullying to stop happening to you.
E. Should bullies receive counseling and at least 6 hours of community service?	E. Bullies should receive counseling and at least 6 hours of community service.
F. Are bullies insecure?	F. Bullies are insecure.
G. Are popularity, power and status most important to be successful today and some of the major reasons for bullying?	G. Popularity, power and status are most important to be successful today and some of the major reasons for bullying.

PREVENTING BULLYING:
A Manual For Teachers In Promoting Global Educational Harmony

H. Are bullying and aggressive behavior learned or are they innate (i.e., biological or part of our character)?	H. Bullying and aggressive behavior are learned and not innate (i.e., biological or part of our character).
I. Will bullying ever end?	I. Bullying will never end. It is a normal part of adolescence and we just must accept it and deal with it in the best way possible.
J. Will respecting and helping others get you far in life?	J. Respecting and helping others will not get you far in life. This is a dog-eat-dog world.
K. Are religious people less aggressive than non-religious people?	K. Religious people are less aggressive than non-religious people.

Agree

Disagree

Activity #36: Give and Receive Compliments

Note: Use this activity near the end of your semester because some students may not feel ready or familiar with others in order to compliment them.

<u>Activity goal:</u> For students to practice giving and receiving compliments to one another. This activity creates a positive and encouraging classroom environment that fosters kindness and friendships versus peer competition, insults or gossiping.

<u>Approximate activity time</u>: 15–20 minutes

<u>Materials required:</u> Copies of the class list, one for each student + teacher; "Student Compliment Checklist" (*provided below*)

<u>Step-by-step activity process:</u>

1. Ask students to define what a *compliment* is.
2. Ask students to give examples of a compliment. (E.g., you're so smart; wow, you look very pretty; you have beautiful hair; you play the piano well; you're a good basketball player; you're very generous; you're funny, etc.)
3. Ask: How does it feel to *get* a compliment? How does it feel to *give* a compliment? Would you like to give and get compliments from everyone in your class?
4. Tell students they will do an activity where everyone in the class will compliment every class, for 2 or 3 weeks, from their peers and teacher.
   <u>Note that</u> it's okay if you're shy or feel uncomfortable. However, complimenting others will make people feel better and you will make more friends that way. If you have nothing to say, you can say, "You have a really nice smile." Avoid just looking at the person blankly and laughing, which might be considered mean.

This exercise teaches you to seek out and see the best in everyone. If you can say something nice to someone you dislike, it can liberate you and allow you to move past it and remember the good things in people.

<u>The point is to say something nice about their character or abilities, not their physical appearances.</u>

5. Make a class list from the sheet provided.
6. Ask students to start complimenting the first person under their name and continue until they have completed everyone on their list.
7. If there is an extra person, tell them to come see you (the teacher).

Optional:

Have a paper stuck on or tied to each student's back. Then have each student write a nice compliment on their back so it's private and confidential.

OR

Have a paper with each student's name on it. Pass the sheets around for everyone to write a compliment on. In the end, return the sheet to the student.

OR

Give a small Ziploc (i.e., sandwich bag) back to each student. Then have each student write a compliment for each of their classmates on a sheet of paper and place it in the bag.

<u>Post-activity discussion questions:</u>

1. What did you learn from this activity?
2. How did it feel to *receive* a compliment? Was it easy, uncomfortable, and why? Do your friends and family often compliment you? Do

you believe what people say? How can you remember what they said? (*Option: write it down.*)
3. How did it feel to give a compliment?
4. What are some reasons that people often do not give compliments?
5. Do you compliment others often? (If not, why? If so, how do you feel when you do?)
6. Do we often remember the good or the bad things that people say about us?
7. How can we remember the good?

Key take-away message:

This activity stresses the importance of giving compliments to show that we value one another. Compliments must be true and sincere. In a classroom community, it is important to promote a caring environment; giving compliments is a way of showing we care for each other. When times are difficult, remember the compliments received here today and know that we have several qualities that are appreciated by our peers and friends.

CHRISTINA THEOPHILOS, M.ED. & RAJU RAMANATHAN, M.TECH

Student Compliment Checklist

For Teacher's Use Only

StudentName	Compliment ☺

Step 7: Encourage Leadership by Getting Students Involved in the Prevention Process

> *"Passing the torch and gift of knowledge fulfills everyone."* — Christina Theophilos

The final step in this student-learning model encourages students to put their knowledge to the test and their imagination to good use. The final activity and/or project is realized when students put what they've learned about anti-bullying into practice by creating a skit, poster, presentation, video, campaign, or even a poem on any topic of their choice. What is important here is for educators to let students be the creators of their projects, which will activate their leadership skills and abilities.

Students need positive role models and authentic leaders that they can look up to and learn from. Youth also need opportunities where they can utilize their strengths and potential. Engaging in leadership initiatives and performing acts of kindness will allow them to focus on doing good for society, rather than focusing inward on themselves or the things they are lacking. Helping others and practicing these mindsets will give students a greater sense of pride and purpose. While students are engaged in these activities, our hope is for students to gain confidence in their abilities, so the use of praise and encouragement is essential at this stage of development.

> *"When you are truly inspired, you will automatically inspire others."* — Datta Yogi Raja

Activity #37: Set Appealing Goals for Their Future

*"Everyone has a purpose in life. A unique gift
or special talent to give to others.*

*And when we blend this unique talent with service to others,
we experience the ecstasy and exultation of our own spirit,
which is the ultimate goal."* — Deepak Chopra

Activity goal: The first part of this activity is for students to complete a writing exercise where they identify their strengths and steps needed to reach their dreams. Students with high, realistic and appealing goals will be empowered to do their best and less likely to go into a depression without having any direction or sense of purpose in their lives. Furthermore, students are encouraged to create a mind-map and movie clip of their future dreams as an additional activity.

Approximate activity time: 50 minutes

Materials required: *My Strengths and Goals* worksheets (provided below)

Step-by-step activity process:

1. Introduce the writing assignment by writing the following question on the board:
   "What are your strengths and future goals?"
2. Distribute the "Cultivating My Strengths and Personal Goals" worksheet (provided below).
3. Inspire your students by having them close their eyes, take a deep breath in, a relaxing breath out, and reflect on the following questions. (Please pause after each question.)
4. Play some inspirational and/or contemplative music in the background, then begin to read the following reflective questions:
   a. Who do you want to be a few years from now?
   b. What do you look like? How do you feel? How is your health?

c. What do you want to see? What do you want to feel and experience?
d. What do you want to taste and learn?
e. Where do you see suffering in the world and how might you be of assistance?
f. What do you have to do now and in the next few years to accomplish these goals?
g. How would achieving these goals make you feel?
h. Take a minute to imagine your life once you accomplish these goals. Allow a smile and a feeling of joy to overflow within you.
i. Now gently open your eyes and begin your worksheet.

5. To initiate the discussion, the teacher can read out some (or all of) the questions provided and give examples associated with his/her own life, so it is authentic and meaningful.
6. Once they are done, ask students if they would like to share their answers with a partner or in small groups of three. If not, tell them to put their strengths and goals in a place where they could see it as a reminder of the bright future ahead of them.
7. Ask students to write down and briefly describe why they (a) deserve these goals and (b) why they're committed to achieving them. (3–5 minutes)
8. Then ask each student to select their 3 most important goals in life and how they hope to accomplish them in the next 3–5 years. (1–2 minutes)
9. Next, have students write the steps they need to achieve these goals? Are they **S.M.A.R.T.** (**S**pecific, **M**easurable, **A**ttainable, **R**ealistic, **T**imeframe) Goals?

<u>Examples:</u>

a. Step 1: I need to get good grades and finish school.
b. Step 2: I need to get a part-time job.
c. Step 3: I need to apply to college.

10. Now pair up students and ask them to share their personal life goals (<u>stress confidentiality and privacy</u>). Allow 10 minutes for this exercise.
11. Once completed, ask each pair to write one reason why it is important to set personal goals. Here are a few examples:
    a. Having personal goals gives you a sense of direction, order, excitement, motivation and quicker results.
    b. Life goals help create your future in advance and help you plan a lifetime of happiness.
    c. Having strong goals helps you break through the bonds of your past while pushing forth towards what you want to do, see, feel, have and become.
12. **Extra:** Have student *draw their future visions or make a movie clip* with inspiring music and images that they would like to see for themselves in the future. These exercises are highly impactful and can assist them towards attaining positive life goals.

<u>Post-activity discussion questions:</u>

1. How did you feel doing this exercise?
2. What are the three most important goals in your life right now?
3. How important is it to plan for your future?
4. What are some realistic ways you can plan for your goals in the next few weeks?
5. What are some factors that might make it difficult or challenging to achieve these goals? Discuss examples:
    a. Having limited funds and the importance of working, saving, and investment.
    b. Fear, low self-esteem, doubt, lack of motivation, etc.
6. What are some solutions and/or prevention strategies for how to avoid or overcome such difficulties?
7. Do you feel closer to identifying certain traits about yourself that can help you become a good leader?
8. Are there areas or people in your life that you think would benefit from your leadership qualities?

Key take-away message:

By completing the worksheet above, students examine their personal values, beliefs and weaknesses. They learn to overcome their shortcomings to achieve the goals they have set for themselves. Through reflection and self-analysis, students bring to light all the traits that will enable them to be ambitious and driven to set meaningful life goals. They are empowered to engage their positive qualities to implement the changes they wish to see in their schools and communities.

Christina Theophilos, M.Ed. & Raju Ramanathan, M.Tech

My Strengths and Personal Goals Worksheet

What are your strengths and skills?

1.

2.

3.

4.

How can you help others with these skills?

1.

2.

3.

Describe yourself positively in 3 words. "I am..."

1.

2.

3.

What are your top 3 personal values?

1.

2.

3.

PREVENTING BULLYING:
A Manual For Teachers In Promoting Global Educational Harmony

What makes your heartbeat? (E.g., What are you passionate about?)

1.

2.

3.

Who would you like to help or impact most in the world or in your community?

1.

2.

3.

What are you most grateful for in your life right now?

1.

2.

3.

What is your (1) definition of happiness and (2) what could you do to be happier right now in your life?

1.

2.

What can you do in school to help others have a positive experience and influence on others?

1.

2.

3.

What are you most proud of that you have done for others in your life?

1.

2.

3.

What are some of your future dreams?

1.

2.

3.

What are your fears/challenges in obtaining these dreams?

1.

2.

3.

What are some things you can do to overcome these fears and challenges?

1.

2.

3.

What are the steps needed to achieve your personal goals?

1.

2.

3.

4.

5.

What are some words of encouragement you can remember when thinking about your goals and why you're absolutely committed to attaining them?

1.

2.

3.

4.

5.

Activity #38: Define Authentic Leadership

"See the light in others and treat them as if that is all you see." — Wayne Dyer

<u>Activity goal:</u> This activity aims to initiate the discussion around leadership by encouraging students to define and express their own positive leadership qualities, in hopes that all students will be authentic leaders and stand up against bullying.

<u>Approximate activity time:</u> 40 minutes

<u>Materials required:</u> Flipchart/blackboard, markers

<u>Step-by-step activity process:</u>

1. Tell students that they will define and discuss the characteristics of being a great leader.
2. Let students:
   a. Sit in a large round circle and complete the sentence: *"I think authentic leadership is…"*
      (Allow some time for students to think and write about their answers.)
   b. Write their definitions on a small piece of paper, read them out loud, and post them on a wall /board as a class collage.
3. Next, have students write the name of their favorite/most respected leader and reasons why they respect them.
4. In groups of four, ask students to brainstorm the main characteristics that each of their leaders possesses.
5. Upon completion, have each group present their list of leadership characteristics while the teacher summarizes them on the board.
6. Thank students for their participation and sit in a large circle to process the activity.

Post-activity discussion questions:

1. How would this world be without great leaders?
2. What would this school be like if we didn't have helpers and great leaders?
3. What leadership characteristics do you possess?
4. How can you practice using some of these skills?
5. What blocks us from being great leaders?
6. How can you use these traits to make a difference in your community, family or school?
7. What does it look like when you respect others?

Key take-away message:

Discussing leadership traits, characteristics and role models is important for students to consider and live up to their full potential. By instilling this inner confidence and leadership skills, we hope students will be strong within themselves, make wise decisions, and help make this world a better place (free from bullying and suffering).

Student Leadership Definitions and Characteristics

Leadership is ...

- Respecting everyone's differences and finding their unique qualities.
- Leading others into positive action.
- Building on a vision.
- Being flexible, non-judgmental, and understanding.
- Having clear management skills that lead to cooperation amongst all workers.
- The ability to adapt himself/herself to make others feel comfortable.
- Speaking in a way that is understood by others.
- Giving jobs/tasks that suit one's capabilities and interests.
- Maximizing the potential of all group members.
- Taking action and never giving up.

- A skill that uses communication and persuasion to organize and achieve goals.
- Achieving harmony among group members.
- Understanding others to better lead a team.
- Encouraging others towards the same goal.
- Promoting love, hope and peace.
- Making a positive change for the betterment of others with love and compassion!

Characteristics of a Great Leader

• Intelligent	• Smart/intelligent
• Loving	• Brave
• Creative	• Confident
• Has a positive attitude	• Passionate
• Shows interest	• Charismatic
• Good communication skills	• Kind
• Patient	• Hopeful
• Good appearance	• Sacrificing
• Open-minded	• Responsible
• Never gives up	• Humorous
• Good speaker	• Honest
• Trustworthy	• Good listener
• Ethical	• Skillful

Activity #39: Get Students Involved in the Prevention **Process**

Activity goal: This activity (or group project) aims at getting students involved in the prevention of bullying. Students will apply what they learned to the real world in order to help motivate or educate others about bullying. Students will practice their leadership skills by presenting their projects to the teacher, class, school or community.

Approximate activity time: 1 hour (or take-home group project)

Materials required: Blackboard/flipchart, markers

Step-by-step activity process:

Part I

1. Begin making a list of the main topics related to bullying. Here are some examples of the topics discussed in this manual:
    - Exclusion and inclusion (non-verbal or emotional bullying)
    - Physical abuse and how to defend yourself
    - Name-calling, body image and self-esteem
    - Healthy relationships
    - Sexting
    - Cyberbullying
    - Respecting diversity (LGBTQ)
    - Racism and discrimination
    - Where bullying is learned
    - Tips on feeling confident
    - Tips on how to make friends and collaborate

Part II

1. Copy, cut and paste the above topics or simply write them by hand, and post them to the wall in separate areas of the room.
2. Ask students to stand up and move to the topic that most interests them for a group project and where they would like to make a difference, versus grouping with close friends.
3. Note that they will be working with new people outside of the regular social peer group in order to make new friends.
4. Once these groups have been formed, ask each team to create a "Group Name" for themselves. This will encourage laughter and team-building skills.
5. Once they have decided on a name, ask each group to share their names and topics for their anti-bullying projects.
6. Tell them to divide roles and the tasks needed to research and put on a PowerPoint (PPT), video, skit or poster up for the school.
7. Upon completion of this, have each group answer the following questions that should be copied on the board, PPT, or ideally copied on a handout for each student:
8. Review each question to ensure clarity.
9. State the time frame given to complete and present their group project. (1–3 weeks is ideal)
10. Allow students some time to work on their projects.
11. Process learning upon completion of each group's presentation.
12. Congratulate their efforts.

Post-activity discussion questions:

1. What did you learn most from this project?
2. What did you learn about yourself and your leadership skills?
3. What new information did you learn about your subject?
4. What do you wish you had to improve on your topic?
5. What are you most proud of regarding your project?
6. What are you most grateful regarding your teammate(s)?
7. What are you taking away from this project into your future?

PREVENTING BULLYING:
A Manual For Teachers In Promoting Global Educational Harmony

Key take-away message:

When students work together and achieve a common goal, there is a need for reward and celebration. I recommend teachers at this final stage to use their imagination and bring candy, or share an inspirational speech expressing your happiness in their efforts and contributions. Note that demonstrating these leadership behaviors is respectable but applying what they learned to real-life situations is even more monumental.

Activity #40: Create an Anti-Bullying Skit — Group Project

Activity goal: For students to get engaged, in an interactive manner, by using their creativity via a skit/movie clip to promote the anti-bullying message.

Approximate activity time: 45 minutes

Materials required: Video recorder

Step-by-step activity process:

1. Inform students that in this exercise, they will be using their creativity to promote the anti-bullying message.
2. Divide the class into groups of 4–5 students.
3. Ask students to think of 1 (optionally 2) bullying scenarios that they have witnessed or heard of and/or they think are the most common.
4. Next, ask students to make a skit showing what targets and bystanders can do to help these bullying situations.
5. Tell students they will demonstrate their skits at the end of class and explain ways the target and bystanders can realistically help themselves.
6. Extra: Use the following bullying examples to save time OR if some groups cannot agree on a situation.
7. Extra: *Videotape each group and show the younger grades.*

Post-activity discussion questions:

1. What did you learn from this activity?
2. What is the best way to deal with bullying?
3. Which team was most realistic?

PREVENTING BULLYING:
A Manual For Teachers In Promoting Global Educational Harmony

<u>Key take-away message:</u>

There are so many forms of bullying, which are all painful and should be stopped. Ways of stopping bullying are to speak up for yourself, don't show your fear or sadness, stand up for each other and talk to an adult. Bullying happens most when an audience is around so standing up for oneself and others are critical to letting everyone know that bullying is not okay. Spreading the message is equally important as students need to be informed about how hurtful bullying can be. Doing it in a creative way that will engage students can be very helpful.

Activity #41: Create Anti-Bullying Posters and Flyers

Activity goal: For students to take initiative and be creative in designing material on how to protect oneself from bullying.

Approximate activity time: 3–4 days (small group project)

Materials required: Computer design software (e.g., Photoshop) or large sheets of paper to design and make a list of solutions for targets of bullying

Step-by-step activity process:

1. Inform students that as an assignment, they will be making posters/flyers or pamphlets on how to protect oneself or respond to bullying.
2. Tell students that their work will be distributed in the school to help students who are being bullied.
3. Note the 5 types of bullying: (1) cyber, (2) sexual, (3) physical, (4) non-verbal and (5) verbal abuse.
4. Divide your class into 5 groups and select a type of bullying for each group.
5. Have them brainstorm solutions on how to effectively handle this type of situation and to do research.
6. Remind students to also include information on who to contact if someone is getting bullied or in trouble.
7. Encourage creativity and teamwork while designing the posters. (*Using the computer to complete their posters is optional for more creative design projects.*)

Post-activity discussion questions:

1. What did you learn from this activity about teamwork and leadership?
2. What did you learn about bullying and how can we all help prevent it?

3. What is the best way to deal with bullying from the posters and messages you promoted?
4. Which team's poster was the most helpful for targets of bullying and why?
5. Where should these posters be hung around school?

<u>Key take-away message:</u>

Getting students involved in the prevention of bullying is one of the best ways of shaping students' young minds into ones of positive leaders. Encouraging teamwork, kindness and cooperation for a great cause is a way in which educators can promote *ethical* thinking and positive behaviors. Don't forget to acknowledge their work, follow up and hang their posters in class or in the bathrooms, lunchroom and hallways.

> *"Watch your thoughts, they become words. Watch your words, they become your actions. Watch your actions, they become habits. Watch your habits, they become character. Watch your character, it becomes your destiny."* — Frank Outlaw

Activity #42: Make an Anti-Bullying Pledge and Certificate of Understanding

Activity Goal: Have students pledge not to bully anyone in or outside of school. Make a collage of all their pledges and stick it on the wall as a reminder of their promise not to hurt or abuse others in any shape or form. (E.g., cyber, physical, excluding others or verbal.)

Approximate activity time: 30 minutes

Step by step activity process:

1. Explain "Make a Pledge" and what that means. Hold them responsible for their actions and note that there are consequences to hurting and bullying others.
2. Distribute the Make a Pledge Form. Play soothing music.
3. Have each student read out loud their pledges and post it to the board as a reminder.

PREVENTING BULLYING:
A Manual For Teachers In Promoting Global Educational Harmony

MAKE A PLEDGE: (Copy and distribute to each student.)

ANTI-BULLYING PLEDGE

I PLEDGE TO (e.g., respect others) …

BY (e.g., showing kindness and compassion) …

BECAUSE … (e.g., everyone deserves to feel safe, confident and happy)

DATE:

STUDENT NAME & SIGNATURE:

Activity #43: Peer Mentoring Program

Activity Goal: Have students from older grades mentor, support and check in with students from younger grades. Assign the older students the task of shadowing, guiding and teaching them life skills during their transition into high school. Since bullying is at its peak during middle school, it is an excellent way for the seniors to guide the younger students about anti-bullying, and simply be there for them and/or intervene if necessary.

Approximate activity time: 50 minutes

Step by step activity process:

1. Assign an older student to mentor a student or a small group of students in a younger grade. Have them meet and discuss school related issues including grades, love, relationships, family life and especially bullying.
2. Encourage older students to act as role models for the school year. Ask them to sit together for 20 minutes over lunch and to prepare questions (*created in groups beforehand*) that will help guide the conversation and check in on students' well-being and happiness.
3. Allow older students to write them a letter about the challenges of school and how to survive during difficult times.
4. Allow students to meet during class hours at least 3 times a year.
5. Encourage older students to exchange numbers and social media information to keep contact with them, or if they ever have a question or problem that they are experiencing related to bullying.

Post-activity discussion questions:

1. What did you learn from this activity about mentorship and leadership?
2. What did you learn about preventing bullying by mentoring someone younger than you?

3. What is the best way to deal with bullying from the posters and messages you promoted?
4. Which team's poster was the most helpful for targets of bullying and why?
5. Where should these posters be hung around school?

Key take-away message:

The message to them is that they are never alone. People care about them and are there to mentor and protect them. Reach out when in need. Support is just around the corner.

A FINAL MESSAGE

The greatest lesson you can teach your students is pro-love and how to build friendships, so our youth do not feel alone in this world. Global educational harmony will occur when we teach children how to meditate inward and heal by helping others.

The way you look at your students and see them in their full potential can impact the future of your students' success. You too, must be calm, balanced, and filled with love and hope for the creation of a peaceful school and class environment.

I pray that these activities are helpful and that we can build transformational leaders helping to create a world free from violence and all forms of bullying.

In summary, you are not just teachers, you are guardian angels helping ease the most important days of our children's critical years of development and self-discovery.

Thank you for trying to make this world a better place and understanding the glory of education.

I hope this manual has served you. Namaste,

Christina & Raju

www.ingramcontent.com/pod-product-compliance
Lightning Source LLC
Chambersburg PA
CBHW030902080526
44589CB00010B/104